A Blueprint for Financial Abundance

GROW YOUR PRO$PERITY MINDSET & CREATE WEALTH

Manoj Kumar

Grow Your Prosperity Mindset and Create Wealth
A Blueprint for Financial Abundance

PEAK PRESS

An Imprint for GracePoint Publishing (www.GracePointPublishing.com)

GracePoint Matrix, LLC
624 S. Cascade Ave, Suite 201
Colorado Springs, CO 80903
www.GracePointMatrix.com
Email: Admin@GracePointMatrix.com

SAN # 991-6032

A Library of Congress Control Number has been requested and is pending.

ISBN: (Paperback) 978-1-955272-35-3
eISBN: 978-1-955272-36-0

Books may be purchased for educational, business, or sales promotional use.
For bulk order requests and price schedule contact:
Orders@GracePointPublishing.com

Disclaimer:

The material in this book represents the opinions of the author and may not be applicable to all situations. Accordingly, the author and publisher assume no responsibility for actions taken by readers based upon advice offered in this book. This book does not offer financial advice, each reader should use caution in applying any material contained in this book to their specific circumstance and should seek the advice of appropriate professionals.

This book material contains advice on entrepreneurship and investing. Please be aware of the federal and state laws and tax regulations when considering the information shared in this book.

Dedication

I am dedicating this book to the Universe and to every human being who impacted my life directly or indirectly. There is a reason I was born on this earth. The universe planned the whole arrangement in such a divine way that I came to be associated with my parents, wife, children, friends, and other human beings.

My life has been transformed due to each and every situation that occurred in my life. *I am thankful to the universe that conspired and gave me the idea to write this book in order to help millions of fellow humans.* I am constantly drawing from the positive energy around me and generating it back to the world. I firmly believe in the fact that each and everything in this universe is a form of energy.

My belief can be explained by the frequency at which I broadcast my demand; the universe receives my command and helps me manifest at the same frequency.

It is important to express my gratitude to those whose books, courses, audios, and videos impacted my life. Some of these mentors are Brian Tracy, Bob Proctor, Sonia Ricotti, John Maxwell, Robin Sharma, Anthony Robbins, Napoleon Hill, Dr. Wayne Dyer, and Dale Carnegie, but there are many others. These mentors have enhanced my experiences and constantly encourage me to stretch my vision and reinforce the notion of seeing the bigger and brighter picture.

A special thanks to Brian Tracy for connecting me to GracePoint Publishing. I wish to acknowledge the outstanding work of the GracePoint team.

My family has encouraged me from day one when I started writing my first self-published book. They have offered me unparalleled support. I am blessed to have parents whose attitude toward life has shaped me more than anything else. Thanks also to my sister Pushpa and my brother Aditya and their families for being supportive of me in one way or another. Finally, I must declare gratitude for the unconditional love from my wife Puja, my daughter Nancy, and my son Omesh. They are a source of genuine joy and limitless ambition for me.

Table of Contents

Preface

I am thankful to the UNIVERSE that conspired and prepared me to write this book. I have always been surprised by the fact that most people openly say, "Money is not everything; money is not important," and the next moment these same people are worried about not having enough money.

In this book, I will help people who want to enjoy a rich life. I genuinely desire to provide guidance to the people who openly declare that they want to have more money. This book will transform a person's mind into a growth mindset, money mindset, and prosperity mindset with the help of my Blueprint for Financial Abundance.

You will be illuminated by the many constructive thoughts poured into the pages of this book. I'll share the answers that I've discovered in my journey to learn how to grow a prosperity mindset and create wealth.

I was born and brought up in India. While India is my motherland, I lived and worked in the United States for six years. Next, I studied and worked in London, England for six years, and that's where my daughter was born. Now I live in Canada, which has become my homeland. My son was born in Vancouver, Canada.

I have lived with and worked with people from all over the world. I came across many wealthy people, some of whom were school dropouts; others were highly educated. I also came across poor people, some of whom were school dropouts; others were highly educated.

Currently, I know a few millionaires with just a basic education, and I know many highly qualified people who are always waiting for the next paycheck to meet their financial obligations.

I love people, and I use money to live a rich life. *For me, money is a medium of exchange for products and services to make my life rich.* I consider money to be a powerful tool, one that is neutral in nature. Money has the power to make a good person even better and a bad person even worse. Money itself is neutral; it is not dirty or evil. Money just expands the quality of the person who possesses it.

I've gained a lot of insights about money by interacting with wealthy people and reading numerous books related to money. Finally, I got inspired to capture my knowledge and insights in the form of this book.

Grow Your Prosperity Mindset and Create Wealth is not merely a book—it is a powerful guide to help people achieve financial freedom. *A prosperity mindset is the power of inner well-being.*

If you have decided to build your House of Prosperity, you must first visualize it using the Blueprint for Financial Abundance and then prepare the plan, including all the distinguishing dreams and goals. In this book, you'll learn how to design your basic prosperity blueprint by integrating mental, physical, and spiritual realms. You'll then start working from the foundational part of this blueprint to make it strong and stable. Next, you'll work on the pillars and then the roof. You'll enthusiastically put the steps in this book into practice for a prosperous life.

As you begin reading, have a firm belief that there is a treasure trove of energy, potential, abilities, desire, and force within you waiting to be harnessed. This book is about redeeming your prosperous life. I describe the Blueprint for Financial Abundance in the first chapter of this book, and I explain it in detail in the subsequent chapters. Read and reread the first few chapters that elaborate on the foundational part of the blueprint. Once the foundation is taken care of, it will be much more fruitful to study and assimilate the subsequent chapters. I will be re-affirming my guidance through repetition here and there as a way to truly anchor in and for others to embody my teachings and approach.

Chapter 1
A Blueprint for Financial Abundance

The universe has already planted all the seeds necessary within you to create a magnificent life. It's your responsibility to carry out the self-improvement and personal growth necessary to harvest the desired fruits of this rich universe. This book will help you to discover your unique potential and bring out the greatness lying dormant within.

My mission is to give you hope that you too can have financial abundance. You can be inspired and motivated only if you have hope. By having hope, you tend to expect an outcome that makes your life more abundant in many ways. This positive expectancy will provide you with the extra cushioning to bear unwanted surprises. Envisioning a prosperous future will motivate you to perform the necessary activities.

If one of your mentors is a multimillionaire and he gives you a blueprint to create a dream life of financial abundance, would you be willing to execute it? If a trusted coach handed you a navigation guide to buried treasure, would you be inspired to follow the guide and do whatever it takes to find the fortune? The Blueprint for Financial

Abundance that you'll meet in these pages is just such a navigation guide.

I am going to show you how to draw a blueprint of your financial abundance, write your own story, and design your destiny. This growth strategy will provide you a winning edge over poverty consciousness. Learning to manifest wealth is the by-product of self-discovery, fruitful activities, the wisdom of being persistent, and the discipline of commitment.

- Do you have the ability to determine what you want, why you want it, and how to achieve it?
- Are you aligned mentally and physically with every action you take?

You are going to learn to develop the mentality of prosperous people in order to play the game of life, to win—and winning is nothing but learning and growing. Ultimately you achieve in accordance with what you become. You need to be highly disciplined, and your inner drive to perform should come from the excitement and exhilaration of doing your best work.

No matter what phase of the journey you are in, you need to be actively involved in the ongoing mental organization and physical momentum. Plan to invest a considerable amount of time to work on your prosperity blueprint so you can manifest your ultimate vision. I have designed this blueprint for your financial abundance, and your duty is to understand it, practice it, and believe that you can achieve a life of prosperity.

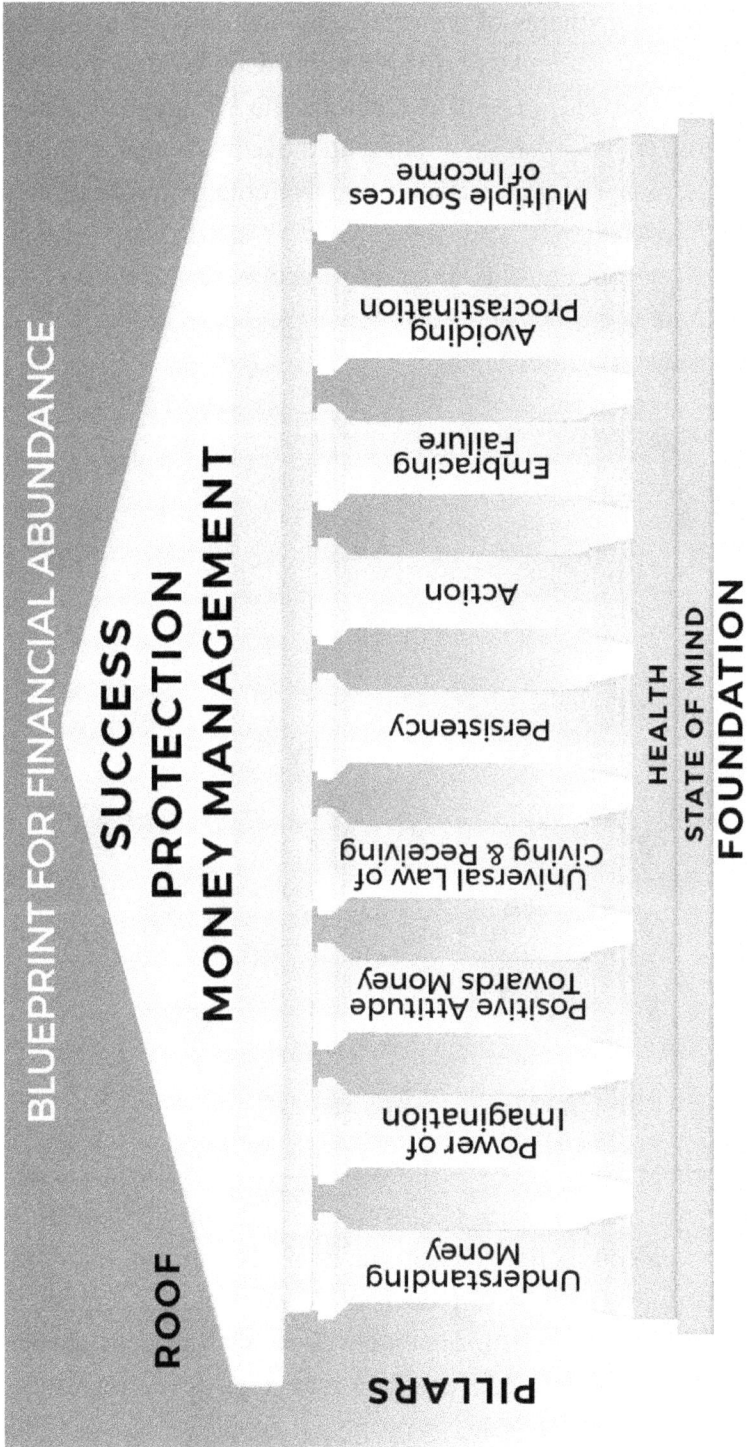

BLUEPRINT FOR FINANCIAL ABUNDANCE

ROOF
SUCCESS
PROTECTION
MONEY MANAGEMENT

PILLARS
Understanding Money
Power of Imagination
Positive Attitude Towards Money
Universal Law of Giving & Receiving
Persistency
Action
Embracing Failure
Avoiding Procrastination
Multiple Sources of Income

FOUNDATION
STATE OF MIND
HEALTH

All the components of the prosperity blueprint are elaborated on in the subsequent chapters. This blueprint will allow you to envision the building process of your prosperous life by putting together the foundation, walls, pillars, and roof with the help of each chapter. Your prosperity blueprint will transport you from the point of origin to the point of destination *if* you repeat your prosperity cycle numerous times in your journey. The prosperity cycle keeps creating phases of achievement and hence helps in renewing and regenerating the energy at every stage of achievement.

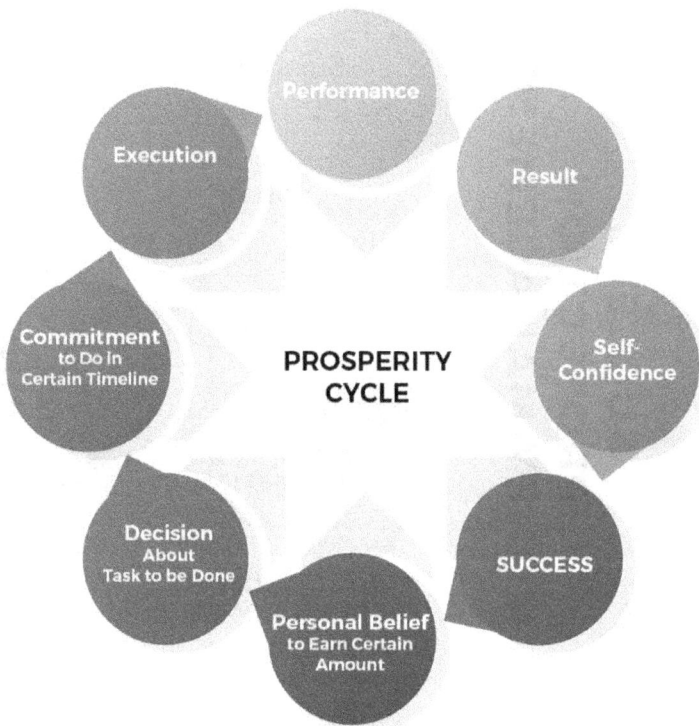

The cycle begins with personal belief. If you believe, then you can achieve. Your belief that you can earn a certain amount of money should be followed by a firm decision to carry out the required work to earn that amount. A firm deadline will create the urgency to achieve your goal. Taking immediate action without any procrastination will lead to the results you desire. A positive outcome acts as a confidence booster, and this plays an important role in achieving success. Once you taste success, whether small or big, your personal belief level will soar. Repeating this prosperity cycle is critical to reaching the destination of an abundant life. Be persistent in following the prosperity blueprint—the longer you persevere, the greater your odds of being prosperous.

Our world is full of wealth, and the universe is abundant with everything imaginable, so why are most people confused and working just to survive? Only a minority are prospering and confident that they can thrive. Most people don't believe in themselves and can't visualize themselves in possession of wealth. Prosperous people seek fulfillment, and they grow so much on a personal level that they often attract riches from all around. Tremendous personal growth doesn't take place overnight, however. Instead, it requires a persistent investment of effort, time, money, and resources.

You will master the art of earning more money once you become self-motivated and self-supervised. You must become a self-starter. Most humans need some sort of supervision or management to carry out their jobs. It's simple logic that supervisors, managers, and leaders are compensated more highly because a portion must go to a worker's superiors if that worker needs to be supervised. This is the reason for different levels in the organizational hierarchy.

When I started working in the hospitality industry, I earned a lesser wage than my supervisor. I had to develop myself to move up to the next level and earn a higher wage. I became a manager solely because I was capable of performing better and was able to lead a team efficiently. As a manager, I earned a higher salary than a supervisor's wage. I wanted to enjoy even more abundance, so I mustered enough strength to start my own business in the hospitality industry. I faced new challenges, new situations, and days filled with extreme ups and downs. I persevered and refused to break down. As a result, I am reaping ongoing rewards in terms of profits, freedom of time, more affordability for my family, contribution to society by creating more jobs, and ongoing support to contractors and other businesses.

People construct their lives based on a series of choices they make, and they are driven to the point their belief level will permit. The prosperous ones are aware and cautious about the quality of their choices. They acknowledge that their choices are the building blocks of their destiny.

The decision to enjoy abundance lies solely with you. You can be prosperous, but you must have your prosperity blueprint in your mind's eye and work every day to construct your dream. You will develop strength and character by doing your part to the fullest. Persist with the belief that you can succeed. The more productive you attempt to be, the more satisfied you will become. A real sense of worthiness comes to you when you utilize your abilities and potential for the achievement of abundance.

Involve the Following Five Processes on Your Journey to an Abundant Life

1. Visualize the kind of life you want to live by imagining your destined future, dream with your eyes open.

2. Make plans by following your prosperity blueprint. Set daily, weekly, monthly, and yearly goals; these targets will give you direction.

3. Develop the habit of being excited and enthusiastic all the time, it will keep you moving forward.

4. Take action before procrastination takes over, one action leads to another, and before you know it, momentum builds.

5. Persevere and don't give up, the realization of any result needs time: you will attain abundance with persistence.

Utilize your ability to control your thoughts and direct them to do the tasks of your prosperity blueprint. Follow through on your prosperity blueprint with determination regardless of setbacks along the way. Remember that setbacks are comebacks and obstacles are your stepping-stones. Prosperity should not be your goal; it should be your state of mind, just like happiness.

Nine Golden Components of a Prosperous Life

1. A healthy state of mind
2. A healthy state of body
3. Healthy relationships with others
4. Choosing faith over fear
5. The Willingness to be thankful all the time
6. Using intention and hope to manifest
7. Self-control
8. The ability to ask the right questions
9. Freedom of time and money

You can design a blueprint to achieve anything in life. Plans might change due to unforeseen circumstances, but the goal can be fulfilled with indomitable courage and faith. There is nothing you cannot do if you set your mind to it. There is great power in focusing on what you can do. You have the ability to inspire one, a few, or many people in this world with the example you set.

Children are inspired by their parents and other heroes. One day in September 2018, my daughter, Nancy, asked me to give her a toonie (a *toonie* is a two-dollar coin in Canada). She was in the second grade. I asked her what she was going to do with a toonie. She answered that she needed it for Toonie for Terry. Kids in her school were helping to raise donations for the Terry Fox Foundation to inspire cancer survivors and researchers.

Nancy didn't know much about Terry Fox, but she knew that he was a brave person and a hero. After little research, I learned about Terry Fox, one of the toughest persons around. Vancouver, situated in the province of British Columbia, Canada, is our hometown. The British Columbia Sports Hall of Fame is located near the main entrance of the BC Place Stadium. The Hall of Fame reflects the history of sporting achievements and there is a special gallery to commemorate the monumental achievements of Terry Fox.

Please allow me to share a brief description of the courage, commitment, faith, and "can do" attitude of Terry Fox in order for you to raise your own power of belief and expectancy. Hopefully, you will be inspired to courageously manifest anything in your life. I hope you will be motivated to follow your Blueprint for Financial Abundance and grow your prosperity mindset.

Terry Fox had a dream of running across Canada. He was born on July 28, 1958, and died of cancer in June 1981, a month before his twenty-third birthday. He lost his right leg to cancer in 1977 when he was nineteen years old. He was an ordinary young man who turned his problematic situation of loss into a victory of faith, courage, and service to others.

Terry decided to run across Canada and ask every Canadian to donate a dollar to raise funds for cancer research. He ran his first half-mile in January 1979, was running twelve miles a day by August, and he began his Marathon of Hope on April 12, 1980. The Canadian Cancer Society agreed to promote the run. He wanted to raise money to find a cure for cancer because he believed that the suffering must stop somewhere.

In the beginning, the Marathon of Hope was nothing more than a van and a man with an artificial leg who hopped as he ran. Only a few people knew who Terry was, but the noble task had begun. At Port aux Basques, Newfoundland, a crowd of ten thousand people pledged ten thousand dollars. The journey gained momentum in the big cities, where thousands became tens and hundreds of thousands.

During his journey, Terry started feeling a bit short of breath. He had pains in his chest and had no idea what they were. Pain and weakness forced Terry to visit the doctor. Eventually, Canada learned that Terry had suffered a recurrence of cancer in his lungs, and the run would have to end. He ran for 143 days and 3,339 miles.

He said, "I want to try the impossible, to show it can be done."[1] There was no thought that he would die. Public sympathy grew for Terry. Donations poured in. This courageous Canadian was soon gone, but his legacy was just beginning. Today over $850 million has been raised for cancer research through the annual Terry Fox Run, held across Canada and around the world. Terry Fox inspired humankind with his example of the human spirit triumphing over adversity.

"The blueprint for success is inside you. It will stay there unless you take it out and create it."[2]

---

[1] https://youtu.be/3BzyHYZgMz8

[2]

https://www.searchquotes.com/quotation/The_blueprint_for_success_is_inside
_you._It_will_stay_there_unless_you_take_it_out_and_create_it./31983/

Chapter 2
Gratitude Brings Riches

An abundance-based mindset allows prosperous people to be in a state of gratitude and rooted to the source. This self-fulfilling habit of being thankful to the people and community attracts more and more blessings. Prosperity is bound to come into your life when you project love and gratitude to the world and start operating with a higher consciousness of abundance, forgiveness, peace, positive creativity, and fearlessness.

As you ponder whether the prosperity mindset is for you, think about your lifestyle. A prosperity mindset involves thinking the right thoughts and then acting on them. You are the only one who is accountable for designing your destiny.

- How well are you performing in the areas of your life that are important to you?

- Are you struggling, surviving, or thriving regarding your financial capabilities?

The majority of people miss out on the psychology behind what it really takes to be financially successful—and this psychology is nothing but the prosperity mindset. The ability to grow a prosperity mindset is a little-known secret for manifesting extraordinary wealth and prosperity.

I love this quote by Zig Ziglar: "Gratitude is the healthiest of all human emotions. The more you express gratitude for what you have, the more likely you will have even more to express gratitude for."[3] Let's relate the essence of this quote to money. No matter what your current financial situation is, feel grateful for the money you have so you will have manifest even more money to be thankful for.

Even if there's a lack of money in your life, you have at least some money to be grateful for. Steve Siebold wrote, "Operating out of a fear and scarcity-based consciousness is playing not to lose strategy, and through the law of attraction acts as a magnet for additional thoughts of fear and scarcity to enter the performer's mind. These thoughts eventually manifest more fear and scarcity on the physical plane."[4]

Here, I will share a short story that illustrates the joy of gratitude. A blind boy sat begging on the side of a busy street. He used his hat to collect the coins and a sign that said: "I am blind—any change will help." His hat had only a few coins. A man who was passing by dropped a few coins into the hat. He talked with the boy, took the sign, and wrote something on the other side of it. He placed the sign so that the new words were visible to everybody. Soon the blind boy realized that a lot more people were dropping coins into his hat. Later that day, the same man came by to talk with the boy again. He asked the boy how it was going. Recognizing the man's voice, the boy asked the man, "What did you write on my sign? Today I have received more money than any other day."

---

[3] https://www.ziglar.com/articles/the-gratitude-journey/

[4] Steve Siebold, *177 Mental Toughness Secrets of the World Class: The Thought Processes, Habits and Philosophies of the Great Ones* (London: London House Press, 2010), 91.

The man replied, "I only wrote your words in a different way." It says, "Today is a beautiful day but I cannot see it." This gave the same message to the people in a more effective way.

The moral of the story is: Be thankful for what you have. Gratitude is the most powerful emotion. Practice expressing thankfulness for what you have. Don't hold yourself back. Just be grateful in all situations, and then you will experience an even better situation.

Never entertain any thought of revenge. Author Wayne Gerard Trotman has rightly said, "Revenge can only be found on the road to self-destruction."[5] Make a habit to forgive; forgiveness is not a sign of weakness. Anne Lamott gave an appropriate analogy by saying that not forgiving is like drinking rat poison and then waiting for the rat to die.

Start taking action regardless of whether you feel like it or not; otherwise, you will end up being like the vast majority of people who are waiting for the right mood to strike them before they act.

Your Prosperous Future Has the Potential to Manifest These Seven Aspects

1. Multiple sources of income
2. Escape from limiting beliefs, guilt, and negative emotions about money
3. Debt-free life
4. Healthy financial habits
5. Quality lifestyle with a dream home, a dream car, and dream vacations
6. Surround yourself with inspiring people
7. Impact others in a positive way with your prosperity

---

[5] https://quotefancy.com/quote/1544934/Wayne-Gerard-Trotman-Revenge-can-only-be-found-on-the-road-to-self-destruction

You can move from poverty consciousness to prosperity consciousness by adopting an attitude of gracious humility. Humility is the human condition of least resistance and a spiritual way to influence people and solicit help from them. Focus your efforts on becoming the kind of person who can attract the things you want out of life. Build your reputation as a person of total integrity who operates from love and abundance.

Negative Emotions About Money

People constantly indulge in activities that do not express gratitude toward money, and thus money goes away from them. Remember, the opposite of riches is poverty, and the actions of not manifesting money will attract poverty.

Eight Examples of Negative Emotions About Money

1. Feeling worried about money
2. Being jealous about others' money
3. Doubting your ability to earn a lot of money
4. Being fearful about losing money
5. Complaining about money to be paid out
6. Feeling scarcity due to the cost of something you cannot afford
7. Arguing about money
8. Getting frustrated about financial struggles

These negative emotions appear when there is a lack of gratitude toward money. The less grateful you are for the money you already have, the less money you will attract.

Gratitude has the power to make you rich and complaining has even more power to drag you toward poverty, as it is evident from the following quote: "Whoever has gratitude will be given more, and he or she will have an abundance. Whoever does not have gratitude, even what he or she has will be taken from him or her."[6]

You might be thinking, "How can I be grateful for money when I am struggling financially?" At this point, I want you to understand that everything starts with your thinking and with your mindset. The person who remains positive, even in challenging situations, will rise above the crowd. So, *nothing will change unless you change your mindset to be grateful for what you have.*

When you think about the products and services you have used in your life so far, you will realize that everything costs money. When you express gratitude for the money you have received so far, you will get ready to receive more prosperity in your future. Some people say that money is not important to them. That's why those people don't have much money and struggle to pay for things they want to have in their life. *If something is not important to you, then the universe will not provide you with much of it.*

Whenever you feel like complaining about something related to money, just remember that complaining attracts scarcity, so, right then and there, flip the switch and creatively express your gratitude toward something about the money you already have. This habit will make you rich and wealthy. The universe will conspire to make you prosperous because of your all-time attitude of gratitude.

When Do People Complain Most About Money?

People complain most when they have to spend money to pay for something. *Any kind of complaint about money creates a situation of scarcity and invites poverty.* Whenever you have to pay out money, release it with joy and be grateful for the goods and services you have received in exchange for the money. Gratitude toward money will enable you to receive more money in your life.

---

[6] Rhonda Byrne, *The Magic* (New York: Atria Books, 2012), 62.

For example, if you have to pay a bill for electricity, don't feel sad or worried, and don't complain. Instead, be thankful that you enjoyed living in light instead of dark, be thankful for the heating or cooling you used, be grateful that you were able to use all the appliances running on electricity, and express gratitude for the people who worked in order to provide you with electricity. Express gratitude for the money you pay out to bring yourself into alignment with the universe and trigger the law of giving and receiving, causing an inflow of money into your life.

Hard work is an important ingredient for being successful in achieving your goals, but it's not a primary factor to enjoy a prosperous life. My parents, relatives, and teachers have always told me that "hard work is the key to riches." This idea about hard work is actually a myth formulated by our dysfunctional society. If this idea would be the deciding factor of financial abundance, then a lot more people would be millionaires because so many people are engaged in sixty to eighty-hour workweeks.

Only a tiny percentage of people who work hard ever actually enjoy financial freedom. Despite all the hustle, most people still have limited resources to manifest the abundance to which they aspire. Hard work can be an essence of success, but only when hard work is executed with the prosperity mindset to the right activities.

Growing a prosperity mindset can be described as programming your thought process regarding your habits and beliefs around money. The inflow and outflow of money in your life is impacted by what you think and do every day. The positive conditioning of thought processes help attract the right opportunities, the right people, and more wealth.

Chapter 3
Health is the Supreme Wealth

Since childhood, we've been told that "health is wealth." Initially, I understood only part of this statement and thought that being physically healthy is the requirement to be wealthy. But later, when my awareness of the world expanded, I realized that physical health plays only a small role in being wealthy. It's mainly mental health that drives physical health and wealth. Mental illness costs a fortune.

It is said that a sound mind lives in a sound body, but it is also true that a sound body can be sustained longer only with the help of a sound mind. An unhealthy person can't work hard to make money, whereas a healthy person can. A person with a healthy body and healthy brain can do everything to attain what they desire. There is a well-known saying: "If wealth is lost, nothing is lost. If health is lost, something is lost. If character is lost, everything is lost."

Health is One of the Most Precious Things in Life

You need to have a sound body and mind to enjoy your wealth. Having any kind of illness won't allow you to perform in a normal way and requires monetary expenses, thus begetting poverty and scarcity. The majority of people take health for granted and only realize the worth of a healthy body when they get sick. When you have any kind of sickness, you want to get well soon; nothing else matters besides regaining your health.

People go to the gym to make their physical bodies healthy. Similarly, people grow mentally tough by working on thought processes. Great physical and mental endurance help us to accomplish tasks more efficiently. A healthy body is like a wall built on the foundation of a healthy mind, and this wall supports the roof of an abundant life. Our physical well-being is interlinked with our emotional and mental states of being.

Anxiety: The Number One Problem of Mental Health[7]

Anxiety and worry go against the universal law of natural existence. Every time you are anxious, worried, and stressed, you yourself become the cause of draining your emotional energy. Worrying is the wrong use of your mind, and it causes disease. It never solves any problem for you, and it is completely disruptive by nature, causing hormonal changes inside your body that eventually lead to physical disorders such as ulcers, abnormal blood pressure, a troublesome heart, weakening of the immune system, thyroid malfunction, headaches, some forms of blindness, etc. Worrying is not only corrosive to the human body, but also to family affairs, personal relations, and business.

Anxiety and fear are cultivated mental health challenges that prevent your mind from working harmoniously with nature. Fear has a tremendous negative effect on humans. Fear disrupts the ability to think and act normally. Fortunately, you can learn to counteract the disruptiveness of fear with faith. Napoleon Hill says, "Faith is a state of mind that may be induced, or created, by affirmation or repeated instructions to the subconscious mind, through the principle of autosuggestion."[8] Practice becoming a person of indomitable faith.

---

[7] https://www.weforum.org/agenda/2019/01/this-is-the-worlds-biggest-mental-health-problem/

[8] Napoleon Hill, *Think and Grow Rich* (New York: Penguin Group, 2005), 46.

Faith mixed with gratitude triggers the accumulation of wealth and creates a prosperous life. Always act with faith and keep fear from ruining your present state of mind.

Any kind of sickness is an indication of disharmony among different states of being. Healing is nothing but the process of restoring natural harmony. Sickness and accidents are the results of imbalance among the physical, emotional, and mental factors.

We have the power to heal ourselves by willingly recognizing the patterns of our feelings and then elevating the vibrations toward awesome feelings and positive beliefs. Using visualization can enhance the healing process of medicine, hospitalization, physio-therapy, yoga, acupuncture, and other methods of treatment. Whether healing is partial or complete, we need to learn to remain happy and hopeful. Personal illness and mass illness or pandemics force us to rest and recover physically and mentally.

We are blessed that our inner mind can create anything we earnestly desire. I am inspired to see myself as a cocreator in this universe. I feel blessed to be a contributor to my own healing as well as to the healing of others. I visualize myself as being a path of least resistance through which universal healing energy constantly flows.

You, too, can refine your thinking and develop a healing consciousness to help yourself and others. A prosperity mindset will not only help you become financially rich but will also help you become solution-oriented in all circumstances. Having a growth mentality, being solution-oriented, and developing a prosperity mindset all play important roles in manifesting abundance in your life.

The universe is abundant, and you can easily harness this abun-dance by being grateful for your health and enjoying an abundance of health yourself. You will enjoy the journey to your abundant life by keeping your body and mind healthy. We often receive a useful message from the universe as a result of illness or misfortune, and we ought to explore within our consciousness the root cause. When we are able to recognize the cause—either by ourselves or with the help of a medical practitioner, counselor, or others—we enter a state of acknowledgment and move toward the process of healing.

A healthy body will provide you with an overwhelming amount of dynamic confidence that will easily impact every other aspect of your life. Zig Ziglar said, "Today be thankful and think how rich you are. Your family is priceless, your time is gold, and your health is wealth."[9] You always live inside your body and mind. Your bodily abode can remain healthy and disease-free only because of your disciplined commitment to eat right, exercise, and treat it as a worship place. A.J. Materi so profoundly expressed it this way: "So many people spend their health gaining wealth, and then have to spend their wealth to regain their health."[10]

By being thankful for your health every day, you attract even more wellness in your life. If you take your health for granted, it will eventually be taken away from you. You need to appreciate something in order to keep, and attract, more of it. With your attitude of gratitude, you are capable of increasing your vitality and energy toward peak performance in your day-to-day activities so you can attract an abundance of everything you desire in your life. Your health is in direct proportion to your level of gratitude, your immunity, your strength, your thought process, your enthusiasm, and the functioning level of your body. Practice visualizing yourself in sound health all the time and affirm that you will always remain full of vitality.

Grow your mindset to feel amazing every day. Never express a lack of gratitude toward the health you enjoy, otherwise this thought of yours will cause even more loss of energy and vigor. We are often amazed at the scientific discoveries of airplanes, cars, bikes, and other means of transportation. But how many times have we realized that our legs and feet are the most precious mode of transportation

---

[9] https://quotefancy.com/quote/943579/Zig-Ziglar-Today-be-thankful-and-think-how-rich-you-are-Your-family-is-priceless-your

[10] https://www.goodreads.com/quotes/6647124-so-many-people-spend-their-health-gaining-wealth-and-then

provided to us by the universe? You can maneuver throughout the day in your home, office, bathroom, kitchen, on the streets, and elsewhere because of your legs and feet. Could you imagine living without legs? So, always be thankful for what you have and for what you can do without depending upon another person! A thankful attitude is essential to maintain your health, increase your vitality, and lift your mood.

Never lose your sense of enthusiasm in any circumstance, bad or good. Practice breeding positive self-esteem to avoid attracting negative feelings of jealousy, fear, and sadness. Fear and doubt can disrupt your happiness, shaping life into an unenjoyable experience. Your ambition of enjoying an abundance of physical health will be fulfilled by maintaining a healthy state of mind. Remember that mental sickness causes various physical diseases.

Become Your Own Healer

Let me explain why it is important to become your own healer. But first, my question to you is: Where do you live all the time?

You might be thinking you spend most of the time at home or the workplace. But I want you to realize that *you always live in your mind and body*. Physically, you might be living in a room, an apartment, or a house, or you might be traveling in a vehicle or staying with your friend or relative, but you are residing in your mind and body all the time. Once you understand and believe this fact, it will be easy for you to heal yourself and attract money.

What does a doctor do? He or she asks about symptoms and problems and then prescribes some remedy or solution.

Likewise, you are needed to assess your state of mind. Find out whether you are giving with pure love, releasing positive energy, vibrating at a higher frequency, or projecting negative energy.

So, as a self-healer, you need to constantly ask yourself this magic question: "How do I feel?" You can ask this probing question several times a day, and only you know the right answer to this question.

Other human beings can just guess how you feel based on your mood or expression.

This self-diagnosis is very important to prepare yourself to become a money magnet. If you feel excellent, good, awesome, lucky, blessed, or relaxed then you are vibrating at high energy and are in a positive state. If you feel sad, worried, or tired, then you are generating negative energy.

John Milton said, "The mind is its own place and in itself, can make a Heaven of Hell, a Hell of Heaven."[11] As soon as you realize that you feel the negative energy in your body, shift the state of your mind immediately. Think good thoughts, do something else—whatever you can to divert your mind from negative to positive thoughts.

Such a mind shift becomes easier by choosing to perceive things differently. Actress Lindsay Wagner says, "When we shift our perception, our experience changes."[12] The name of the game is to practice projecting positive energy all the time. The universe will help you to prosper only when you begin healing yourself. The healing starts from becoming aware of your feelings and then changing your state of mind from a low vibration to a higher vibration.

Don't feel defeated if you catch yourself with low energy. Recognize the fact that as a human, you will fluctuate between negative and positive frequencies, but the important thing is how quickly you are able to take yourself out of a negative mood and start generating positive energy. This shift in your mindset will transform you into a magnet for positive things.

Money will come to you in increasing amounts from various sources on a continuous basis. There will be a continuous flow of abundance because you will be wise enough to remove the blockages

---

[11] https://www.brainyquote.com/quotes/john_milton_110201
[12] https://www.brainyquote.com/quotes/lindsay_wagner_685942

from your life by shifting yourself into a state of gratitude and happiness.

Here are three rituals you can practice so you can heal yourself and transform your life dramatically.

1) Have an attitude of gratitude.

There is always something to be grateful for, regardless of what's going on in your life. Your life becomes awesome when you cultivate an attitude of gratitude. Be thankful for everything you have in your life. *Don't take anything for granted because this attitude equals a lack of gratitude and leads to the loss of what you have.*

The habit of expressing thankfulness tends to eliminate feelings of anger and other negative emotions. An attitude of gratitude will help you attract prosperity and abundance. Good health is also a by-product of being grateful.

2) Watch your association.

Entrepreneur Jim Rohn said, "You are the average of the five people you spend the most time with."[13] Since you are reading this book, you likely want to become rich and wealthy. In order to achieve financial freedom, you need to associate with people who make a lot of money and are fulfilled with money. You have the ability to dream about what type of person you want to become, and then you have the power to pick and choose to be around people who are already successful.

People in your circle of influence should be at a higher level of vibration and more successful than you. Every time you want to elevate your financial situation, upgrade your circle of influence. Make the effort to go outside your current circle and current comfort zone to find people more fulfilled than you.

---

[13] https://www.goodreads.com/quotes/1798-you-are-the-average-of-the-five-people-you-spend

You can change your association by reading books written by successful people, attending events, and joining networking groups. At the same time, it's important to guard yourself against negative people who have a poor mindset. Their lower vibration about money and prosperity will bring your energy level down.

Your new circle of influence is important because positive and successful people have the intention of uplifting others and encouraging others to move toward prosperity. Watch your association and constantly upgrade it by moving out of your comfort zone; people vibrating at a higher level will strengthen you in every aspect and will always believe in your big dreams.

If you want to become a millionaire, go and find a few millionaires. Spend time with them and study how they think, what they believe, and how they do things. You will be amazed at how positive they are. They believe in taking calculated risks. They like dreaming big, and they believe in their dreams. *Successful people have the habit of stepping out of their comfort zone and taking massive action to accomplish their goals.*

3) Believe in the universal law.

The law of giving and receiving, the law of cause and effect, and the law of sowing and reaping all have almost the same meaning. You need to do the first part, and the universe will take care of the second part in various ways. Just keep doing the right thing as per your plan, keep making progress, and be persistent. Have patience and be present to receive the blessings when the time comes.

Often people do work for a while, and if they don't see any result, they give up. Remember, the winner never quits, and the quitter never wins.

Chapter 4
Wealth is a State of Mind

Human beings are emotional creatures. Emotions are the drivers of human behaviors. You were born on this earth with a right to have freedom—that's why you deserve financial freedom. Emotionally, you need to be tuned in to see the positive side of everything, and this will help you to persevere and flourish. Andrew Young rightly said, "I have about concluded that wealth is a state of mind, and that anyone can acquire a wealthy state of mind by thinking rich thoughts."[14]

People become wealthy because they expect to become wealthy. Become a deliberate originator of your thoughts and focus on nothing but prosperity, riches, abundance, happiness, joy, and peace. Positive expectation is self-discipline born out of desire and strengthened with positive self-talk. The discipline of creating autosuggestion or mental programming will make you prosperous long before you are wealthy in reality. Visualization has great power and leads to realization. Goethe, the German philosopher, put it this way: "Before you can do something you must first be something."[15]

---

[14] https://www.brainyquote.com/quotes/andrew_young_146779

[15] https://www.azquotes.com/quote/589171

You can expect to have all the money you need to fulfill your vision of a prosperous life, but you must take responsibility for creating your abundant life. *Remember that this responsibility is taken, not given.* By developing the discipline of prosperity thinking, you will attract abundance throughout your life. This process involves learning and growing continuously. Prosperity allows you to live a rich and fulfilling life. The goal to enjoy a prosperous life draws focused attention to move you in the direction of abundance.

Author Napoleon Hill said, "More gold has been mined from the thoughts of man than has ever been taken from the earth."[16] The one critical factor that separates prosperous people from destitute people is their dominant thinking. You have been thinking so many thoughts anyway, so why not think about prosperity? Prosperity thinking leads to a growth mindset and focuses on solutions rather than problems.

The skill of prosperity thinking can be learned. When you make the effort to change your thinking and become a prosperity thinker, you are making the very best investment for your future. A change in your thinking pattern doesn't take place overnight. It is a process of flooding your thinking continuously with good stuff. Dominant thinking all day long should be strengthened with faith and oriented toward abundance, hope, prosperity, and happiness.

People develop a poor mindset over time based on a strong belief that they will not have enough money. They then only feel comfortable associating with others who also have a poverty mentality. They have a difficult time breaking the cycle of poverty in their family. Only an elite few make an effort to grow a prosperity mindset and seek growth-minded people to hang out with.

Here are fifteen common differences between a poverty mindset person and a prosperity mindset person:

---

[16] https://www.brainyquote.com/quotes/napoleon_hill_152865

Poverty Mindset	Prosperity Mindset
tries to earn money	creates wealth.
attracts fear	attracts growth.
prefers safety	prefers growth over safety.
avoids risk	tolerates and rises above risk.
creates an illusion	creates its own reality.
dwells in the comfort zone	dwells in the effort zone.
thinks about scarcity	thinks about abundance.
wants to *have* first	wants to *become* and then *have*.
has a tendency to blame	loves to take responsibility.
is frustrating	is fascinating.
is ungrateful	has an attitude of gratitude.
is problem-oriented	is solution-oriented.
stops learning	believes in lifelong learning.
is infected with ego	is humble.
lacks vision	dreams, imagines, and visualizes.

Rich people think differently, do things differently, and rise above the crowd. The universe helps those who take responsibility to help themselves and others. While people with a poverty mindset worry about poor economic conditions, people with a prosperity mindset spend time upgrading their skills and knowledge in their chosen field. A prosperity mindset helps people create a better personal financial situation through competence and inner drive.

The Process of Becoming a Prosperity Thinker Relies on the Following Four Aspects

1. **The influence of good thoughts:** Follow the law of sowing and reaping; remember that what goes into your head will

come out. Therefore, it is important to constantly keep yourself under the influence of good thoughts. Good thoughts are energy and ideas captured in good audios, motivational videos, self-help books, and uplifting groups on social media. You have the ability to use these tools that have the power to stimulate your thinking.

2. **The influence of prosperity thinkers:** Surround yourself with prosperity thinkers and eventually you will start generating thoughts powered by abundance and happiness. The people you choose to spend time with have a great impact on your thinking and behavior.

3. **The influence of intention:** The intention to think positive, good thoughts is highly required from you. Your intention starts the transformation of prosperity thinking. The efficient way of being intentional is by becoming accountable to yourself. Have the discipline to regularly expose yourself to seeds of prosperous thoughts. Your intention will breed your thoughts.

4. **The influence of action:** Henri-Louis Bergson wrote, "Think like a man of action—act like a man of thought." Action involves motion. Action has the ability to move. Action injects life into thinking. Implement any idea you have to generate revenue, help others, or create opportunities. Your initial motion will lead to momentum, and momentum leads to materialization.

Our association with others, news about the nation's economy, personal past experiences, and others' approval all play a great role in programming our minds. Most people's minds are programmed to think small. Small thinking doesn't lead to the necessary action to support big results. Big thinking demands massive action, which in turn leads to great results.

There is no virtue in being content with just enough money to live another day or barely having enough to pay your bills every month.

Almost everybody wants more money, but the majority settle for a lot less. Most people compromise too much and don't live a truly fulfilled life.

You can practice focused thinking about abundance by avoiding cluttered thinking and not allowing your mind to hop from one thing to another. Give your attention to the activities that have the potential to produce good results. Spend your time thinking in a way that removes distractions about the small stuff. When you decide to go up the ladder of a rich and fulfilling life, you should be mentally prepared to give up the little things.

If you are experiencing financial lack, it's time for you to decide, commit, and take action to change your situation. The universe will conspire to provide you with all those things you pay attention to. You should always have the right intention and a positive attitude toward the things you want.

Any negative attitude related to money will take money away from you. Develop the ability to identify the beliefs that repel money away from you. Nobody else will do this for you. Only you are responsible for taking charge of your beliefs and attitudes toward money. It's time to upgrade your thought process about having a lot of money.

The Power of Circulation

As you breathe in and out, air circulates in your body. In the same way, blood circulates constantly in your body to keep you alive. Money should also circulate freely in your life, as well as in our nation's economy. Blockages of any type lead to sickness physically, mentally, or economically.

Here is a short story that explains the effects of circulation and stagnancy in nature. The Dead Sea and the Sea of Galilee are both located in Israel. These two water bodies are fed by the Jordan River. But these two seas differ from each other based on what they do with the water that flows into them. Water flows into the Sea of Galilee and flows out of it, causing the water to circulate. This sea is alive and supports an abundance of fish, birds, plants, and people. On the other hand, no water flows out of the Dead Sea. The water stays stagnant and evaporates to increase the salt content of the water. Without any water circulating, the Dead Sea is unfit to support any life forms. No fish, birds, plants, or any other living thing can survive in the vicinity of the Dead Sea.

Many people act like the Dead Sea with respect to the circulation of money in their lives. If you don't experience the constant circulation of money in your life, then there is a problem with your attitude toward money. You can build fortunes and bless yourself and others by dealing with the money per the universal law. When you get sick physically, you seek medical advice for a remedy. Likewise, if your life is prevalent with scarcity, you must fix your mental perspective toward money.

Research has proved that your own words have the power to program your mindset and thinking. An affirmation is a kind of statement that declares something to be true. Positive affirmations have the ability to reinforce constructive and growth-oriented thoughts in the brain.

Affirm the statements that would not create any conflict in your mind around your beliefs and feelings. If you have the daily affirmation "I am wealthy," but you are poor, it might create contradictions. Harmony in your mind will occur by affirming statements like "I am becoming richer every day," "I am on my way to prosperity," "My wealth is increasing daily," "I am getting healthier every day," "My business is growing every day," and "I am moving toward financial freedom."

When self-confidence and personal belief about your big dream start developing, it will then be desirable to affirm boldly with statements like "I am wealthy," "I am prosperous," etc. *It's important to find ways to be positive without creating any kind of opposition in your mind.* Harmony creates a receptive situation.

By visualizing the end result, the mind has the ability to develop the willpower and belief to realize that goal. *Develop the habit of imagining, seeing, and feeling the reality of becoming rich.* Learn to live with a growth mindset. Again, remember that you always dwell in your own mind, no matter where you find yourself physically. That's why it's so important to live with wealth consciousness. This state of mind is attained by constantly repeating and believing that money circulates freely in your life, just like blood circulates in your body.

Have an idea, sustain it, and have faith in it until imagination becomes conviction. This is the process of fulfilling any desire. *Never magnetize your mind with fear and doubt.* Have faith in the universal way of realizing your dreams. The more specific your desire gets, the more dynamic it becomes.

The universal law of *cause and effect* continuously operates in our lives. Our outward actions are related to our inner feelings and convictions. Your outer body, circumstances, and financial situation are the results of inner beliefs and thought processes on a daily basis. Your habitual dominant thought creates your beliefs. Inner belief is responsible for how you act in the outer world. With the profound knowledge that your inner being creates your outer world, always remind yourself to be happy, and then you will manifest happy circumstances.

Becoming the master of your thought process empowers you to control everything outside of you. Believe that and behave as if you can have everything you wish to fulfill. Have faith in the universal law and take action to achieve your goal.

Positive thoughts ignited with feelings will move you from dreaming to doing. *Magnetize your mind with faith that you are destined to be wealthy.* Become wealth-conscious to create wealth. If you are envious of another person's progress, it means that your mind is charged with fear. This negative state of mind can quickly lead to your downfall.

A scarcity belief has no positive power. By indulging in the act of cheating others, a person ends up defrauding himself or herself. A scarcity mindset attracts loss in different forms. Those who have accumulated money the wrong way end up paying a huge price by losing their peace of mind, being fearful, or becoming sick.

Condemning others' wealth is primarily stealing from oneself. Outer forces take away your wealth only if your mind is occupied with fear, worry, and jealousy. Don't entertain thoughts of poverty and failure; whatever you feel, is what you tend to attract. Faith and fear signal two actions of an opposite nature. One drives you toward freedom, while the other drags you down toward self-imprisonment. You can stop this downward spiral by prayer, which is a psychological practice of replacing fear with faith.

Complaining about one's own financial situation, rising prices, or bills to be paid and condemning others' prosperity constitute a mighty negative force. This invisible, toxic concoction of condemnation and complaint acts as a sword to cut your link with the source of abundance. You can't receive something without any kind of connection with the creator or provider.

Whenever you pay for something, release your money with joy; it will return to you multiplied in magnificent ways. *Rejoice in the abundance of others. Feel good about others' happiness.* This will allow you to prosper faster.

The true nature of life is progressive—whatever people achieve, they want more of. People with a growth mindset understand that a person's safety and security are found within their thought process and their ability to perform. That's why they don't sacrifice growth for safety and constantly perform to achieve a higher state of abundance.

Your desire for abundance indicates that you have the urge to grow and accomplish your dreams. You are born to grow, but you should also learn to enjoy what you have in the present. You can live your dream by taking planned actions persistently.

Your constructive opinions mixed with positive feelings lead to actions that attract happiness, health, and opulence. *A growth mindset is the state of prosperity consciousness.* Joseph Murphy wrote:

> Whatever the mind dwells upon, it multiplies, magnifies, and causes it to grow until finally, the mind becomes qualified with the new state of consciousness.[17]

> Whatever your conscious mind assumes and believes to be true, your subconscious mind will accept and bring to pass. Believe in good fortune, divine guidance, right action, and all the blessings of life.[18]

Attaining a new, higher state of consciousness should be your daily goal. This is the secret leading to all growth, all discoveries, and all achievement. A new, higher state is attained by constantly entertaining positive, dominant thoughts.

Decluttering limiting beliefs, doubts, and unhappiness from your mind is required if you want to experience feelings of well-being, success, and harmony. It's your personal right to pick and choose the type of thoughts you desire to entertain consciously. Your mental state of faith and confidence has the ability to materialize strong desires of fulfillment.

In order to ward off negative thoughts, constantly repeat positive affirmations. *Daily repetitions of positive affirmations magnetize your mind with expectancy and faith.*

---

[17] Dr. Joseph Murphy, *Riches Now* (London: G&D Media, 2020).

[18] Joseph Murphy, *The Power of Your Subconscious Mind* (New York: Prentice Hall Press, 2000), 33.

Chapter 5
Understanding Money

It's very important to have an understanding of money. *Most people are not richly compensated with money because they silently or openly criticize, complain about, or condemn money.* If you are jealous of someone wealthier than you, if you refer to rich people as greedy, if you think that money is bad, and so on, then you are broadcasting negative energy signals. The universe obeys all commands, and in this case, it will ensure that you don't attract more money.

"Money is neither good nor bad; it is energy. It is the way money is used that determines whether or not it is a positive energy that will benefit you and others." [19] Money is nothing but a medium of exchange. The amount of money represents the value of a product or service. *Money is just a symbol and a convenient mode of exchange for something.* People will give you money in exchange for something from you.

---

[19] Sanaya Roman and Duane Packer, *Creating Money: Attracting Abundance* (Tiburon, CA: H J Kramer Inc., 1988), 230.

Always remember, you attract what you praise, and you lose what you condemn. Never, ever consider money to be bad or evil. *Money is a neutral symbol.* Money tends to bring forth the innate nature, or quality, of a person. Good people perform more good deeds with extra money, whereas bad people do the opposite with extra money. Prosperous people utilize wealth to help themselves and other people, without becoming attached to their money.

Never use money as a tool of manipulation. It's up to you whether you use fire to cook your food or torch somebody's house. It's your decision to either use money to enjoy the finest things in your life or give it to someone to kill another person. T. Harv Eker says:

"Money is not going to make you good or bad. Money is simply a tool, just like a hammer. A hammer can be used to build or to destroy."[20]

It's in your ability to have a fulfilled life by using money with the right intentions. Your love of money should not render you blind toward other aspects of life, thus leading to disillusionment. Truly prosperous people have all the money they want while still possessing a mindset of peace, harmony, and love.

You can choose to become more valuable or less valuable. People who are focused on finding solutions become highly valuable and attract lots of money. People in the habit of complaining about problems lose their value and thus have very little left to exchange for money. Everyone has the equal privilege to live a rich life. It's all about personal decisions and choices.

---

[20] T. Harv Eker, *The Good Millionaire* (Bellingham, WA, 2019), 46.

Chapter 6
Harness the Power of Imagination

Your secret to becoming prosperous is your imagination. Your ability to imagine is the superpower of your magnificent mind. When people desiring prosperity imagine their abundant future, they create an image of an abundant situation. Then they visualize the image so vividly and so frequently that they have the feeling of ownership of that future image. The habit of creative visualization breeds mental harmony and fosters happy feelings, thereby broadcasting the positive energy required to take action.

Imagination empowers you to dig deep for possible solutions to worldly problems, align the information, and formulate the desired results. No matter which part of the world you come from, you will perform according to what you imagine to be true about yourself and your surroundings. Upgrade your belief system, upgrade your imagination, and upgrade your results. Be solution-oriented and you will be wealthy and prosperous.

What is most lacking in the journey from poverty to riches is the ability to create a crystal-clear image and develop a vision of the thing one desires. Do you really believe that you are prosperous—or that you will become prosperous? If yes, then you are. If not, then first elevate your belief level. If you can't relate to the fact that you will manifest an abundance of wealth, then practice having a feeling of abundance by telling yourself that the world has abundant air, abundant water, abundant sunshine, abundant natural resources, abundant wealth, etc. Treat your mind as a resourceful mine from which you can extract limitless riches through the tool of your imagination.

The sooner you become conscious of abundance, the faster you will attract prosperity. Stretch your thinking. Associate with people, read books, listen to audio, watch videos, and spend time in nature— all of which can inspire you with new ideas. Be ready to be stimulated, start working, and persist no matter what. It's your time to commit, so be determined to do it. Abundance is just around the corner, but you must not waver or quit.

Inspiring Thoughts on Imagination

- "Imagination is more important than knowledge. Knowledge is limited. Imagination encircles the world."[21] Albert Einstein
- "The man who has no imagination has no wings" [22] Muhammad Ali
- "What is now proved was once only imagined."[23] William Blake
- "You can't depend on your eyes when your imagination is out of focus."[24] Mark Twain

---

[21] https://quoteinvestigator.com/2013/01/01/einstein-imagination/

[22] https://www.brainyquote.com/quotes/muhammad_ali_163702

[23] https://www.goodreads.com/quotes/103931-what-is-now-proved-was-once-only-imagined

[24] https://www.brainyquote.com/quotes/mark_twain_131203

- "Imagination is the beginning of creation. You imagine what you desire, you will what you imagine, and at last, you create what you will."[25] George Bernard Shaw

- "The imagination is the golden pathway to everywhere."[26] Terence McKenna

- "If you fall in love with the imagination, you understand that it is a free spirit. It will go anywhere, and it can do anything."[27] Alice Walker

- "To bring anything into your life, imagine that it's already there."[28] Richard Bach

Your ability to concentrate your energy on one dream at a time will help you to develop an imaginative thought process. Images of prosperity and abundance, when nurtured constantly in your mind, *will* materialize. Universal law demands that these positive images be regularly energized with feelings of happiness and joy.

[25] https://www.brainyquote.com/quotes/george_bernard_shaw_113045

[26] https://www.brainyquote.com/quotes/terence_mckenna_475793

[27] https://www.brainyquote.com/quotes/alice_walker_625848

[28] https://www.brainyquote.com/quotes/richard_bach_383522

Chapter 7
Get Rid of Negative Energy Toward Money

Creating a prosperity mindset involves rewiring your habits, attitudes, thought patterns, and beliefs toward money. You will become a money magnet by possessing a prosperity mindset. It is very important to create a positive image of money in your mind upon which you can act to fulfill your financial goals. This chapter will help you to declutter your mind and get rid of any negative energy toward money.

We are surrounded by visible things and invisible energy at the same time. Invisible energy is always more powerful—and more difficult to control. It's vital to train yourself to grow a prosperity mindset so you can harness the invisible energy working in your favor.

Be happy, excited, and open-minded when it comes to learning about the process of becoming rich. Your decision to read this book proves that you are among the small percentage of people who do something significant to attract money into their lives. Irrespective of your current relationship with money, the principles in this book will shift your belief about money in a positive way, allowing you to start behaving differently to achieve financial abundance.

A scarcity of money is similar to a disease. Many people are born poor and many of them work to cure this disease of poverty. Some of them develop a prosperity consciousness and become wealthy. Every human being has the right to completely unfold materially. There are rich people in every country, and many of them were not born rich.

Rarely do thoughts arise completely developed. Almost every time, our thoughts need to be shaped until they manifest. It's always better to write down prosperity thoughts on paper. Putting your thoughts and ideas on paper injects energy into them instantly, and they last longer. S.I. Hayakawa once said, "Learning to write is learning to think. You don't know anything clearly unless you can state it in writing."[29]

Many people are jealous of others' wealth. Many condemn others' growth. Most people complain about financial difficulties. Many complain about their current jobs. If you want to become rich, start choosing the thoughts that attract money. Don't allow yourself to be influenced by scarcity messages about money and richness. As Mike Todd says, "Being broke is a temporary situation. Being poor is a state of mind."[30]

People stay poor because they have a poor people's mindset. However, you are a champion because you chose to change your financial situation by taking action and reading this book. The universal law of action and reaction will definitely produce positive results toward manifesting money.

Financial transformation will not happen overnight. It's a process. By reading this book and understanding and implementing the concepts in real life, you will become a money magnet. It's your moment to move forward money-wise.

---

[29] https://quotefancy.com/quote/1229740/S-I-Hayakawa-Learning-to-write-is-learning-to-think-You-don-t-know-anything-clearly
[30] https://www.brainyquote.com/quotes/mike_todd_392262

You have stepped on the path to financial freedom. Financial abundance is the destination, and you can enjoy the journey. You are capable of earning a lot of money. You need to develop the mindset and aspire to be rich and wealthy.

It's important that you become specific about money. How much do you want to make? Don't settle for less. Think and write the big amount that has the capacity to accommodate all your dreams and goals. Decide by what date you want that money. Do not worry about how. I am going to show you how. Don't be fearful about thinking about one million or many millions. Everything is possible!

I'm here to reinforce the belief that you can acquire hundreds of thousands or even millions. If one person can do it, so can you. You were born rich. My duty is to make you aware of your mental richness, which you can't see quite yet. Remember, the invisible is always more powerful than the visible. Wealth is nothing but the by-product of your state of mind.

Many human beings have achieved total financial freedom, so why not you? My mission is to help you acquire the right perspective about money. You have to learn to perform the way others do who have created a lot of wealth. I know the difference between living a life of scarcity and a life of abundance; I have lived both. I can guarantee you that there is a lot of joy and peace when money is the last thing you worry about. Many of you might be in debt. I was also in debt at one point, but I have turned it around—and so can you.

I witnessed a lot of poverty in my early childhood. I grew up walking, running, and playing barefoot. But fortunately, my parents were hardworking people who tried their best to provide a good education for their children. They made a lot of sacrifices and had to borrow money to pay for my first year of college.

I started my career working in a fast-food restaurant. I did not have access to an adequate amount of water on a daily basis. I had to stand in a long queue to collect one bucket of water every day. I had to use this water for drinking, taking baths, washing my clothes, and so on.

When I moved to Mumbai for a better opportunity, I didn't have enough money for a place to live. One of my friends worked in an office in the city, and because he was a good friend of the business owner, I was allowed to sleep on the floor for two nights after everybody left for the day. It was a one-room office without any attached bathroom. Early in the morning, I woke up to use the paid outside toilet located not far from the office. After two days, I managed to connect with some of my college mates and they allowed me to stay in their rented house, so I started sharing the rent with them. This was a godsend for me starting in the big city.

Next, I took a job working as a waiter on a casino ship in Florida. I got my visa and flew to Miami along with three others from Mumbai. On reaching the Miami airport, we were picked up by our agent. He was supposed to take us to the ship, but he told us that there were no jobs at that time, and we would have to wait. He put us up in a room in a cheap hotel in downtown Miami and left.

We had only a few Indian currencies between us, which we decided to convert into US dollars. On conversion, the four of us had about forty-five dollars combined. We were told that it could take more than a week before we could start working on the ship. Until that time, we needed to spend our own money to feed ourselves. We ended up eating bread, butter, jam, and a little bit of milk as our breakfast, lunch, and dinner.

It was a difficult and sad situation. We were living in a situation we did not expect. I'm telling you all this because I want to assure you that *we all have our own share of hardship.*

The bottom line is that I had decided at an early age that I deserved financial freedom in my life. And so do you. So, if you're having financial difficulty, I urge you to decide and commit to being rich in your mind first.

As I have mentioned before in this book, the most powerful way to visualize yourself as wealthy is to start associating with rich people and studying their mindset. This can be done by reading their books or watching their videos. These people can be alive or dead. You get to decide who you'd like to emulate.

I associate this way with rich people every day although I have never met them and some of them have departed this world. People like Napoleon Hill, Dale Carnegie, Earl Nightingale, Brian Tracy, T. Harv Eker, John C. Maxwell, and Bob Proctor, have influenced my thought process and actions magnificently.

It's your right to be rich and wealthy. Do exactly what successful people do, and you'll be successful too. Sow the right seeds and begin nurturing them. Start thinking like the wealthy, acting like the wealthy, and doing what the wealthy do. Begin experiencing a wealthy lifestyle in your mind. Remember, *visualization is realization.*

A Reality Check

It's important to recognize the following four consequences of a lack of money in your life:

1. A lack of money brings insecurity to your life.

2. Scarcity creates instability.

3. Financial struggles crush your dreams. When you can't afford what you need and you are in debt, you live an insecure life. This creates more negative talk in your mind, which eventually materializes in your life.

4. Monetary problems draw your attention mainly toward your own survival. When you are facing serious financial challenges, you become self-centered. You are constantly thinking about your situation. Even if you want to, this prevents you from helping others most of the time.

As Lang Hancock said, "The best way to help the poor is not to become one of them."[31]

So, it is wrong to say that money is not important. You are not meant to live a life of scarcity because of a lack of money. *If you say you don't care about money, it really means you are ordering money not to come into your life.* The universe will receive your scarcity signal and will work in a way to make sure you don't receive enough.

It's stressful and toxic when you don't have enough money to pay your bills or buy enough food for your family. This leads to an increase of negative energy internally as well as externally. If you want to enjoy your life and help others, then make it your priority to be free of financial hardships. You need to think, plan, and take massive action to earn money, save money, and grow money.

Let's Talk About a Few Outcomes of Manifesting Financial Freedom

- You gain more confidence in yourself by having more money. If you enjoy financial freedom, you dare to have bigger dreams and goals. You are always excited about life. Money is the last thing you worry about when you wake up in the morning. You get ideas and have the strength to act on those ideas.

- You have more opportunities to help others by having more money. When you have an abundance of money, you automatically become less self-centered. When you don't worry about yourself, you can focus more on others. You will find many ways of helping others when you don't stress about your own financial condition.

Prosperity enables you to spread positive energy in a bigger way. A lack of money affects all other areas of life—family, marriage, work, and community. When you have financial freedom, your

---

[31] https://economics.org.au/2011/10/the-best-way-to-help-the-poor-is-not-to-become-one-of-them-lang-hancock/

positive energy makes it easy to thrive in this world. Negative energy generated due to scarcity is very toxic and has the power to spoil relationships with other people around you.

It's important for you to have financial freedom and keep your positive energy high so you can be a source of greatness for others. Positive vibrations in your life automatically attract positive people and situations into your life.

Let's see how your happiness is related to your financial situation right now. If you believe that you will be happy when you will have financial freedom, if you are thinking that you will be joyful when you will be debt-free, then it means you are not happy in the present. You can neither go back to live in the past nor can you live in the future. All you have is the present, and you can be either miserable or happy. You can only live in the present.

Jim Rohn said, "Happiness is not something you postpone for the future; it is something you design for the present."[32] If you shift your mindset, you can actually experience joy and happiness right now about the abundance that will materialize in your future. I advise you to practice experiencing prosperity right now. Make it your ritual to experience abundance in the present moment. This habit will provide you with the right momentum to achieve financial freedom faster.

What Is Real Prosperity?

Real prosperity is not external but internal. An actual sense of fulfillment comes from inside. The correct mindset of thinking and experiencing great stuff in the present creates true abundance. Most people complain about their past or are worried about their future; however, they fail to realize that all they have is the present moment. You have the power to act in the moment and do something about it right now. The past and future exist only in your mind.

---

[32] https://www.brainyquote.com/quotes/jim_rohn_147498

Currently, you are learning from this book about money and mindset. You don't have any problems right now, instead, you have a blessing in this moment to realize that you can do wonders in the coming days.

Feelings of scarcity occur only when you're thinking about the lack of money. You have a choice to turn this around by brainstorming on things that can create more income for you. There are hundreds of ways to add new income and create abundance. *But everything starts from your thinking and acting positively right now.*

Albert Einstein wisely said, "We cannot solve our problems with the same thinking we used when we created them."[33] You cannot solve any problem by staying at the same level or living in the past when the problem occurred. You need to elevate yourself to a higher level to find a solution. You can generate positive energy by conditioning yourself to be happy. Learning to be enthusiastic helps you to elevate your energy, and this pushes you out of any challenging condition.

The future has only one meaning for us. Set your goals, determine your destination, and visualize all the good things you want to have in your future. The future is for visualizing only good and great stuff. You have the ability to plan now, act now, and change your direction now. You have the blessing of starting now toward your future destination. Never entertain worrisome thoughts on your way to future realization.

I strongly encourage you to shift your mindset toward prosperity. I urge you not to live with a poor-people mindset. Cultivate a growth mindset instead. I truly believe you can fine-tune your energy frequency to a higher vibration.

Whatever kind of frequency you release, the universe will receive your signal and then will provide you with the matching manifest-

---

[33] https://www.brainyquote.com/quotes/albert_einstein_121993

ation. The universal law of cause and effect will make sure that your visualization becomes your realization.

What Is Your Visualization of Money? Why Do You Desire More Money?

Visualization is a way of transmitting your imagination to your body and subconscious mind as signals or commands. As you practice visualization techniques, you will become skilled at attracting prosperity and achieving imaginative end results.

Take a moment to answer this question: What will happen when you receive more money?

Your answer should clarify two aspects of why you want more money. The first aspect is *tangible* (i.e., what you will exchange that money for). And the second aspect is *intangible* (i.e., how you will feel after spending your money to receive something).

I really want you to energize your two answers. You might want to write down the questions and answers and share them with someone else in your family or with a good friend.

- First, what will you do with more money?
- Second, how will you feel after doing what you wanted to do with the money?

You might want more money so you can pay off all your debts or buy your dream car or move into your own house or go on your ideal vacation. You can have more than one answer as to what you will do with more money. My goal here is to provide you with clarity. Be specific about why you want more money.

The next thing is how you will feel once you have done what you wanted with the money. How would you describe your mental state? How will you experience that moment of achievement? You will probably have a greater sense of security and happiness. You will probably feel more confident, or you might feel very excited. These are all states of mind. So, actually, you want more money to be secure, happy, confident, or excited.

Did it help to provide more clarity about the end result? What is the nature of the final thing that you want because of money? Were you able to identify as tangible or intangible?

Most people keep thinking about the tangible objects they want to buy, and this quest for material things is never-ending. The tragedy of life is that so many people don't realize that they can be happy or confident or stress-free even before acquiring the physical things they desire. You can experience the intangible without having visible things. You can visualize the invisible even without seeing it. Harry Emerson Fosdick taught that if you hold a picture of yourself in your mind's eye long enough and steadily enough, you will be drawn toward it. A fulfilling lifestyle begins with an image vividly held in your mind as you visualize yourself enjoying the abundance of the universe.

Becoming wealthy and living a rich life is nothing but a higher state of mind. You can have less money and still be happy—or you can be very wealthy and still be sad. So, I strongly urge you to put yourself in a state of happiness. This will accelerate the materialization of your dreams. Your state of positive vibration will make it easy for you to think clearly and take massive action with enthusiasm toward your goals and dreams.

If your monetary situation is the only thing that's not ideal right now, then you should be thankful that you have other things in your favor. You can turn your financial situation around by making firm decisions, staying committed to what you are supposed to do, and being persistent.

Every situation in your life is temporary unless you choose to make it permanent. You were born rich. You were born to be a winner. Decide, commit, act, and finish. Don't give up on your dreams and goals. Be persistent and never quit.

I'll leave you with one task now to finish this chapter and help you implement what you have learned so far. Your task is to write down your affirmation. Have your daily affirmation written on paper and always carry it with you. You also can keep it in sight in different places in your home or car. The goal is for your mind to accept and absorb the essence of your daily affirmation.

Here is my own affirmation:

The universe always supports me. I am grateful to have a growth mindset. I am blessed with good health, abundance, and prosperity. I love people and use money. I am happy to release any money, and it comes to me in increasing amounts on a continuous basis from various sources.

You can use my affirmation or create your own affirmation. Daily affirmations have great power in transferring messages to your subconscious mind. The subconscious mind then works nonstop to transmute your desires into physical reality.

Chapter 8
The Mental Switch for Wealth

Do you belong to that group of people who want the same richness in life that prosperous people enjoy yet are mentally not ready to perform and work for those riches?

In this chapter, I will discuss the mental switch that will help you change your current financial situation into a more abundant and fulfilled condition. A positive attitude toward money is the switch that starts your journey to a fulfilling life. Your attitude determines how well you are positioned on the way to prosperity and happiness. Work on improving your mental approach to money by talking yourself into prosperity consciousness. The rich and elite are open-minded about learning the concepts and strategies that will enrich their lives; they are peak performers in their chosen fields.

If you depend on others to plan your life, your destiny will not be designed according to you. You have the power to make anything doable by planning, and you can do anything by taking that first step. If you fail to plan, you are planning to fail.

You can rewire your belief system to be prosperous by changing the words you use while talking to yourself and others. Using encouraging, positive, and uplifting language helps program your prosperity mindset. People with a prosperity mindset are self-motivated and their own inner drive keeps them moving forward. They prefer burning out rather than rusting out, and they usually take less rest than they actually need in the early stage of transformation.

Prosperous people raise their level of consciousness by being attracted to the education and awareness of wealth creation. If a person operating in poverty consciousness wins a lottery worth millions of dollars, he eventually will find a way to make it back to the middle class or even fall back into poverty. This is primarily because they don't raise their self-image and they don't upgrade their self-talk regarding their economic situation. Nobody else is responsible for any situation in your life except you. Being disciplined to make growth plans according to your circumstances will orient you toward optimism and solutions.

Ten Reasons Optimism Leads to Prosperity

1. An optimistic attitude increases your belief level and hence produces higher vibrational energy that leads to prosperity.

2. Possibility thinking places you in a position to materialize more things and experience abundance.

3. When you are optimistic, you become aware of many other possibilities.

4. Optimism enables you to attract opportunities you never thought of.

5. You draw cooperation from other people, and your journey to prosperity becomes enjoyable.

6. Optimism allows you to visualize a bright future and dream big.

7. Optimism magnifies your potential and capabilities.

8. Optimism breeds a winning instinct inside your mind.

9. Optimism prevents you from quitting your dreams.

10. Optimism develops an outlook that stops justifying any situation as being impossible.

How Do You Feel about Your Current Financial Situation?

Are you in bad shape? In an average situation? Satisfied or experiencing really good stuff? My intention is to make you feel awesome with excellent outcomes regarding your financial situation. I want you to understand and believe that your financial condition is nothing but the materialization of your mindset about money.

The universe requires you to change your inner thought process about money in order to transform your financial situation forever. Your capacity to have money, use money, and enjoy money is in direct correlation to the way you think about money.

Claire Boothe Luce said, "Money can't buy happiness, but it can make you awfully comfortable while you're being miserable."[34]

Either you make money, or you make excuses—you can't make both. It doesn't matter how many good opportunities you have in your life; unless and until you decide to take action to earn extra money, nothing will happen. Don't worry about failing. Don't get addicted to the approval of others. Just keep going; keep bouncing back again and again until you succeed.

As soon as you start appreciating wealth in its many forms, you will develop a new mindset of attracting wealth from various sources on a continuous basis in your life. Begin appreciating others' prosperity and stop condemning others' wealth in order to welcome wealth and prosperity in your own life.

People with prosperity mindsets create such an intense level of focus to realize their dreams, that they overcome all the challenges they encounter. They program their subconscious minds to believe their financial dreams are a reality, and they adopt new behaviors that

---

[34] https://www.goodreads.com/quotes/53130-money-can-t-buy-happiness-but-it-can-make-you-awfully

are congruent with this new reality. They believe that prosperity lies in the constant process of learning, growing, and becoming rather than in a single occurrence of having. They develop and solidify abundance-empowering beliefs primarily through their own limitless self-talk. Ralph Waldo Emerson said, "Nothing external to you has any power over you."[35]

Shift your poor person mentality to a rich person mindset. This is a key ingredient to your transformational process. Wealthy people are capable of connecting the dots to the source of abundance through their thoughts and deeds. Start loving people and using money—not the opposite. You need to believe that money is a good servant, and you need a lot of it to be served properly. Money will constantly flow into your life from other people in exchange for something you provide.

Reality Check

Answer these five questions:

1. What do you *think* about money?

2. How do you *feel* about money?

3. Do you believe that money should come to you continuously?

4. Why should you have a lot of money?

5. Do you believe that you can help more people by becoming rich and wealthy?

The fact is, what you think and visualize about money will dictate your capacity to materialize it. When I started thinking about money positively in every way, my mindset transformed me into a money magnet. This chapter will help you to shift your mindset. But in the end, how soon you absorb the wisdom given here and take yourself to the next level of fulfillment with money all depends upon you and only you.

---

[35] https://www.goodreads.com/quotes/48870-nothing-external-to-you-has-any-power-over-you

If you don't have the amount of money you want, this is mostly the result of your limiting belief around money. Your belief can be compared to the frequency with which you are broadcasting your demand for money; the universe receives your command and helps you manifest at the same frequency. Astrophysicist Neil deGrasse Tyson tweeted, "The Universe is under no obligation to make sense to you."[36] The prime hindrance to your path to prosperity is self-doubt and worry—both are disruptive and corrosive.

So, I encourage you to tune up your thinking frequency and cultivate a wealth mindset. The shift from a poor person mindset to a rich person mindset will miraculously affect your financial condition in a positive way. Pay attention to what you are thinking and saying. You might be speaking words on a daily basis that are placing you in the very situation you want to avoid.

For example, if you say, "I don't have enough money," the energy of your words ends up making this true. The universal law of attraction will work in your favor and make sure you don't have enough. Instead, you need to train yourself to say positive words and statements. For example, you might say, "I am on my way to prosperity," which is the opposite of scarcity. And then the universe will conspire to make you prosper.

Four Common Myths about Money

Myth 1: It's Hard for Me to Earn a Lot of Money

Do you believe that it's hard for you to earn a lot of money? Do you recognize the similarities and differences between poor people and rich people?

Poor people and rich people live in the same country. They have the same number of hours in a day. But they think differently and have different values to offer in exchange for money. They know that you

---

[36] https://twitter.com/neiltyson/status/1378387351806820357

don't get paid for your time; you receive money in exchange for the value of the product or service you provide.

Get rid of any limiting beliefs you may have and start believing that you can earn a lot of money—and then start doing the things that increase your worth. Once you start seeing yourself as a more valuable person, others will find you more valuable too. This process will enable you to manifest more money in the same number of hours.

I will make it easy for you to understand. It's a *myth* to think that it's hard for you to earn a lot of money. The *fact* is that it's easy for you to earn lots of money once you begin believing in yourself, behaving like a rich person, dreaming big, and doing whatever it takes to achieve your goals.

Myth 2: I Don't Have What It Takes to Be Wealthy

Whatever you think of yourself will always be true, so why don't you start believing in yourself? If so, many people can be rich and wealthy, why can't you? This universe doesn't discriminate between you and anyone else. You are the only one who has the power to change your perception about yourself—nobody else. You can escape the hindrance of a scarcity mindset by enthusiastically endeavoring to live joyfully. You achieve this by carrying out your dynamic purpose fueled with a burning desire.

Start believing and behaving like the wealthy. Start dreaming and doing things the way they do. Becoming prosperous has nothing to do with your education, color, race, sex, or any other external factor. Abundance is the by-product of your state of mind and your productive habits.

You can be wealthy in any kind of economy and at any age once you decide to become wealthy. The only obstacles on the way to becoming rich are your own limiting beliefs. Whatever your condition and circumstances, consider them as stepping-stones to success and take the leap of faith to gain momentum in your journey to financial freedom. Everybody has the option to convert obstacles into stepping-stones to success and a rich life.

Myth 3: Money Is Evil

Money is neither good nor bad. Money is just a neutral symbol used as a medium of exchange. There are poor people who are good, and there are poor people who are bad. There are rich people who are good, and there are rich people who are bad. There are spiritual people who are rich, and there are spiritual people who are struggling financially.

Will Smith said, "Money and success don't change people; they merely amplify what is already there."[37] I view money as the power that makes you more of what you are. Let's assume that you are a nice person, but poor. Once you become rich, you will become an even nicer person and will be able to help many other people—which you are unable to do now because of financial challenges.

In another scenario, let's assume that you are a bad person, but poor. Once you become rich, you will become an even worse person, and you will start using your money to do things that will bring misery to others.

It's wise to view money as a powerful tool and become a money magnet in every possible way. Money will help you to connect with the source of power, and you will become more of what you are now.

Myth 4: I Need to Work Hard to Become Wealthy

My question to you is: Aren't you working hard now?

I would say that most people are working very hard anyway. Irrespective of the nature of a job or business, most people work hard. Doctors, cleaners, nurses, teachers, cooks, waiters, construction workers, and office goers are all working hard.

Everybody is singing the same song. "Oh, I work so hard, but I still do not have any money left at the end of the month! Oh, I work very hard, but I cannot get out of debt!" In order to be wealthy, you have to sing a different song. You have to work differently. Yes, in

---

[37] https://www.brainyquote.com/quotes/will_smith_167216

the beginning, you'll need to work hard. Then, once you gain momentum, you will begin to enjoy the freedom of both time and money. Remember, whether you are rich or poor, you will always have the same number of hours in a day.

You need to do exactly what rich people do. Learn to multiply your hours; learn to multiply the number of hands working for you and with you. *Learn to automate your tasks, delegate the tasks which cannot be automated, and spend your time doing what only you can do.*

I elevated my financial situation, and you can too. Find out what you want to do for the rest of your life, then find out how people become rich. Next, learn about successful people in your chosen field. Set your goal. Be clear about the price you are willing to pay to become successful. Make a plan and take massive, consistent action. Don't give up—be persistent. As renowned coach Vince Lombardi said, "Winners never quit and quitters never win."[38]

Whatever you choose to do, it should be able to provide you with the opportunity of creating passive income. Passive income requires little or no active involvement to generate ongoing revenue. Active income is generated by hands-on involvement in doing something. Active income will never make you wealthy. Active income is usually just enough for survival. But by working hard in the beginning, you can create passive income. Passive income makes you wealthy and provides you with freedom of time and money.

By now you should be competent enough to point out your own limiting beliefs and get rid of them in order to make room for more constructive beliefs. Remember, you have access to that remote control which can flip the switch from a negative to a positive mindset instantaneously. It takes constant practice, and you can also return again and again to this book until it becomes second nature.

---

[38] https://www.brainyquote.com/quotes/vince_lombardi_122285

What else will happen once you develop your growth mindset? You will be able to take responsibility for everything in your life without any complaint. You will have ownership of your situation. Because of your mental strength, you will be able to turn bad times into good times. You will be unstoppable!

You may remember this famous quote by Sophie Tucker: "I've been rich, and I've been poor. Rich is better!"[39] I encourage you to focus on being rich and happy. Happiness will follow you and you will feel more secure when you have more money in your bank account. Financial fulfillment provides more security and stability in your life.

A change of mindset requires a change in beliefs and thought processes. You can act as your own money doctor; you can diagnose your own limiting beliefs around money and start converting them into positive beliefs. When you visit a doctor, you describe your symptoms, and the doctor asks you a series of questions to uncover the real problem. Once a diagnosis is made, treatment can start. The treatment for any sickness should be specific, not merely guesswork.

Let's say you are struggling with money, or you want a lot more than what you have right now. I've provided some specific questions for you to answer. The most effective way is to write your answers on a piece of paper or in a journal. Writing down your answers will enable you to realize the true nature of your beliefs and your words about money.

- What do you think about your friends or relatives who are very rich?

- What are your thoughts when you see a stranger driving a very expensive car?

- When you see a beautiful home, can you see yourself owning a similar or better house?

---

[39] https://www.brainyquote.com/quotes/sophie_tucker_145824

- When you eat at a restaurant, do you check the price and then decide what you are going to order?

- How would you feel if you were financially free and never had to worry about money?

- What kind of thoughts come to your mind about your rich friends?

- Do you condemn and criticize others' wealth and success?

- Do you visualize yourself as capable enough to become wealthy?

- When you see someone driving an expensive car, do you think he or she is just showing off?

- Do you have the confidence and belief that you are on your way to financial freedom?

Once you have written down your answers, compare them with the explanations given here. Your answers to these questions will allow you to become aware of your thought process around money.

Complaining about money attracts poverty, and gratitude toward money attracts prosperity and abundance. Every time you come across a negative belief, immediately shift your thinking to positive. In the beginning it will take a lot of effort, but by the time you've read this book multiple times, it will become a habit of yours to uncover your limiting belief around money and shift it quickly.

Even if there are opportunities for you to earn money in various ways, your negative thoughts and limiting beliefs will not allow you to receive the money. So, it's primarily up to you how fast you trans-form your mindset about money. Recognize each and every limiting belief that you have about money and get rid of it.

Start appreciating others' success. Be grateful for what you have, and you will attract more. Flood your mind with joyful thoughts about money and start feeling good about the things you will get in exchange for your wealth. Start visualizing the joy and happiness that will come into your life when you have a greater sense of security, prosperity, and abundance.

Chapter 9
The Universal Law of Giving and Receiving

In this chapter, I will discuss the important universal law of giving and receiving. We'll cover the various aspects of this universal truth, and I'll show how you can implement certain things into your daily life in order to attract more money. For instance, one of the habits of manifesting a prosperity consciousness is giving without expecting anything in return. Prosperity consciousness itself will attract more abundance into your life. The process of giving becomes easy when you become aware that the source of supply is unlimited, and the universe operates from total abundance.

The Definition and Interpretation of the Universal Law

The law of giving and receiving functions in a similar way to the law of sowing and reaping. This universal law simply means that any current situation of yours is the result of your past actions, and your present actions will determine your future results. Our universe operates based on a balanced flow of energy. The universal law of giving and receiving proves the ongoing exchange of energy in various forms. This law can also be referred to as the law of cause and effect.

One Universal Law—Three Different Forms

1. The law of sowing and reaping

2. The law of cause and effect

3. The law of giving and receiving

Since you are here to learn how to make lots of money, please pay attention to the universal law. From this moment on, remind yourself of the following statement: "I am happy that money is constantly circulating in my life." You will be happy when you release money, and it returns to you multiplied. *Always have an attitude of gratitude while paying for goods and services.*

The universe doesn't discriminate between humans; it works impartially for everyone. Success or failure is the result of the decisions made and actions taken; it has nothing to do with good luck or bad luck. *The harder you work, the more attempts you make, and the more you persevere, the luckier you become by increasing your probabilities.*

You can't reap what you haven't sown. How can you expect any result or reaction without an action? When you plant a tree, it doesn't bear fruit in a few days; you typically need to wait years. Similarly, there is no shortcut to becoming rich. Too many people want to get rich quickly. Even if they succeed, they won't be rich for long. Getting rich and staying rich is the result of a prosperity mindset. Become disciplined enough to pay the price for what you want and attract abundance. The price often includes the pain of delayed gratification. Avoid searching for instant pleasure so you don't fall into the trap of regret. Jim Rohn said, "Discipline weighs ounces, while regret weighs tons."[40]

---

[40] https://quotefancy.com/quote/837926/Jim-Rohn-Discipline-weighs-ounces-and-regret-weighs-tons

Becoming fulfilled in life is attained by focusing on the cause, discovering the purpose, and heartily performing to the best of your ability. Bigger causes always result in bigger effects. Ralph Waldo Emerson once said, "Shallow men believe in luck. Strong men believe in cause and effect."[41] When you focus on the effect, you might succeed in acquiring some money; however, the absence of a greater cause won't allow you to experience a fulfilled life. Those who focus only on the effect operate with a poverty mindset and are fearful of scarcity. They don't fully enjoy what they do.

When the going gets tough, the poverty mindset tells you to back off from a goal or task. On the other hand, the prosperity mindset inspires you to draw strength from emotional power, reminds you about the cause you are working for, and propels you to move forward consistently toward your vision of attaining prosperity.

A prosperity mindset ignores physical and psychological pain; it considers this temporary and recognizes that the cause is worth fighting for to achieve the result of abundance and fulfillment. Any kind of success is achieved as a result of overcoming struggles along the way.

It's time for you to believe in universal law and start attracting money. When you give, you receive. The more you give, the more you receive; it's important to help others. Usually, when you are facing financial difficulties, you tend to think more about your own situation than about helping others.

But whenever you go out of your way to help others, you feel good, and great things will start happening in your life too. However, make sure you help others with the right intention without making it obvious that you are doing something for somebody. Just help others with joy. This will elevate your positive vibration, which will be received by the universe and returned to you multiplied.

_____

[41] https://www.brainyquote.com/quotes/ralph_waldo_emerson_121133

The universal law works only when your intention is right, and you are giving with pure love. You don't give with the intention of receiving more; instead, you give with the pure intention of helping others. Also, when you help someone, you will not necessarily receive from the same person. Money and other good things may come to you from different people in different forms.

But the law of giving and receiving works continuously. So, just help others and don't worry about making a note of it; the universe is constantly working to make sure the law is followed. John D. Rockefeller Jr. said, "Think of giving not as a duty but as a privilege."[42]

Money is not the only thing you can give. If you have money to spare, that's awesome; otherwise, there are many other ways to help others. You should expect to experience joy and love by helping others. You can help with money, donate food, give a gift, support a cause, or give away something others need. You can help people you know or even strangers. Giving can take place in cash or kindness. Money isn't the only thing you have to give.

When you help others with the right intention, your positive vibrations are elevated to a higher frequency, and good things start flowing freely into your life. The law of attraction overtakes the law of giving and receiving. The law of cause and effect begins to show up.

You need to put consistent effort in agreement with the universal law toward achieving your goals and dreams. Persistence is the character trait that keeps you glued to abundance forever.

Anything that happens in your life happens for a reason. Never question what happens; your duty is simply to take responsibility for whatever happens. Never say, "Why did this happen to me?" Instead, say, "This happened *for* me."

---

[42] https://www.brainyquote.com/quotes/john_d_rockefeller_jr_338777

Because you are currently learning and assimilating the true meaning of the universal law, it shows that you desire better results in your life. Therefore, you are above the crowd. What does the crowd focus on? The crowd wants to change an effect or is worried about what they reap. But you have the huge privilege from now on to become aware of changing your cause instead of changing your effect. When you change your cause, the effect will automatically be different.

The universe has conspired to place you where you are, reading these words, *right now*. From this moment on, you will focus on sowing good so you also will be reaping good. Practice giving and helping others with a positive intention, and don't forget to give to yourself with love and pride. Practice releasing money with joy to pay for any goods or services at your disposal.

Whether you are spending money for a service to yourself or buying groceries or new clothes, paying a bill, or helping others, in each instance release the money with gratitude and happiness. This higher vibration will allow the money to return to you multiplied from different sources.

Never feel guilty for spending money on yourself, but at the same time, you should be able to differentiate between the right use of money and wasting money. You always deserve to receive from yourself with love, and this intention works at a higher vibration. Joy, love, and happiness are always associated with positive energy.

Any kind of helping others will place you in the position to receive. Become prosperity conscious. Always look for ways to give with love. You are the only one who can elevate your vibration around money. Money is a form of energy, and you allow this energy to circulate in your life through the law of giving and receiving.

Lower vibration or negative energy will not make you receptive to prosperity and abundance. Scarcity is not good for you nor for others around you. A negative mindset is like a deadly virus. It is invisible and highly toxic. It creates scarcity, worry, and fear. As

Robert Zoellick said, "There are many roads to prosperity, but one must be taken. Inaction leads nowhere."[43] Work hard to have healthy mental growth, then do something to earn money.

As we end this chapter, I challenge you to help at least one person every single day. You will benefit according to the law of giving and receiving by helping a fellow human being. The kindness you pass on will multiply. Helping others makes you feel good and connects you to the source of abundance.

Thirteen Ways You Can Help Others

1. Expressing your gratitude to others is the most important way you can help others and yourself. You can do it verbally, write a note, send an email, or by using social media.

2. Be friendly. You can make someone feel a little better by being friendly or projecting a smile.

3. Always look for something to appreciate about someone. Appreciating someone in public is even better.

4. Donate money randomly with pure pleasure for a worthy cause.

5. Donate something other than money. Others might appreciate the stuff you don't need anymore.

6. Volunteer your time to help a charity.

7. Occasionally you might come across someone in need of help. Ask what you can do and then do it if you can.

8. Teach someone something you know. You can teach a child or an elderly person. Teaching or coaching is a noble form of giving.

9. Feed a hungry person. Giving money to homeless people is often not recommended because you don't know if it is going

---

[43] https://www.brainyquote.com/quotes/robert_zoellick_643925

to be used for alcohol or drugs. Instead buying food and showing respect is a good gesture.

10. Listen to someone who is depressed or frustrated. Sometimes people feel better by just talking to someone. Be generous and lend your ears.

11. You can also lend your voice. Sometimes a person needs someone to speak up for him or her. You can speak up by yourself or join others for the right cause.

12. Often being patient is a gesture of help. A person might have difficulty understanding, doing, or learning something.

13. Help by doing a chore like mowing a lawn, removing snow for an elderly person, or cleaning a house.

You can come up with many more ways to help others. Just help in whatever ways you can, and the universe will help you in amazing ways. Keep doing your part and keep helping others without waiting for results.

Performing your duty is in your hands but getting results and attracting rewards depend on many other things. Have faith in the universe. Everything will be taken care of at the right time. JUST DO YOUR PART AND BE HAPPY!

Chapter 10
Self-Control and Persistence

You must practice self-control to have a disciplined life. I often tell myself, "Self-control is the ultimate tool to discipline myself and align my actions with my prosperity blueprint." A positive attitude, excitement, and self-motivation are the necessary tools to overcome worrisome situations. Have self-confidence beyond all doubts that you will prosper. Develop mastery over your mind by continuously exercising self-control and willpower. Let your mind become obedient to your prosperity blueprint rather than allowing it to be in control of your unfruitful habits.

No one should ever think of living in this world without working; idleness is the chief cause of all negative situations. Laziness is corrosive. Ignore all external objections and self-doubts trying to drag you toward poverty. Samuel Johnson once said, "Nothing will ever be attempted if all possible objections must first be overcome."[44] Use the power of uplifting talks and autosuggestion guided by positive affirmations to overcome doubts and fear. Dominate your thinking with faith and confidence.

One of the important characteristics of personal prosperity is perseverance. The world is full of talented, educated people who are

---

[44] https://www.brainyquote.com/quotes/samuel_johnson_122057

unsuccessful. I would say the reason is not the shortage of opportunity in this world but the absence of purpose and a lack of persistence in people. Most people are ready to quit when they don't get the results they hope for after a while. Persistence provides you with staying power and doggedness, enabling you to bounce back from life's turbulence.

Don't become a professional instant pleasure seeker. Learn to delay gratification by constructively working on your plan to achieve your prosperity goals. Be one of the few tough ones who persevere a bit more and strike the goldmine. Society will consider you lucky without realizing that the harder and longer you persist, the luckier you become. Thomas Edison said, "Genius is one percent inspiration and ninety-nine percent perspiration."[45] Perseverance develops strength and draws the world's wealth within your reach.

The repetition of good thoughts and actions counteracts the corrosive effects of contrary suggestions. Practice creating wealth and lift yourself out of the turmoil of poverty into the pinnacle of prosperity. Resolution is a common quality most prosperous people possess and this allows them to make exhaustive use of their abilities.

Persistence brings you prosperity, following up brings you fortune, and staying power makes you successful. *Be willing to persist and you will prosper.* Persist in rewiring your prosperity mindset by incorporating corresponding habits, beliefs, and actions to empower yourself.

Five Steps Involved in the Process of Rewiring Your Prosperity Mindset

1. Believe that you will realize abundance in all areas of your life.

2. Upgrade your self-talk and use uplifting language while speaking.

3. Activate your energy by adding physical movements and actions to your task.

4. Visualize in advance what you seek to realize.

5. Be happy and blissful all the time.

---

[45] https://www.brainyquote.com/quotes/thomas_a_edison_109928

Chapter 11
Interpretation of Success

Success as defined by the dictionary is the achieving of results wanted or hoped for. Success means different things to different people. A sports champion can be seen as successful in the chosen sport but not as an actor; an artist can be seen as a success in the field of art but not as a researcher; a famous surgeon can be seen as a success in the medical arena but not in the engineering field.

Success is the progressive realization of a specific cause by a specific person. Success is relative to a person's worthy goal. The law of attraction operates without any bias for positive or negative. Whatever you think about most of the time, you attract in your life.

You can be successful in creating a truly fulfilled life after developing balance among these four aspects: physical, mental, social, and spiritual. You can develop a habit of succeeding by turning your goal into a burning desire with excitement and enthusiasm. Become a ferocious aspiring creator of your dream destiny. Develop a burning desire to prosper, and you will achieve prosperity.

Winning is a habit, and so is quitting. Success is addictive, and so is failure. Winning must be constantly exercised for the sake of keeping success-habits in practice. You can overcome all the setbacks, and you can succeed in being prosperous with sustained action.

The universe has the tendency to abundantly reward success-oriented people with a multitude of opportunities. These people have the clarity that their choice to dream big, their ability to take massive action, and their quality to persevere can potentially catapult them into the arena of the rich, wealthy, and prosperous. Avoid playing the game of life safely to be secure and comfortable. Start shooting for growth which lies in the effort zone, not in the comfort zone. Every setback develops achievement muscles and helps you to bounce back.

Eighteen Personal Reminders to Successfully Stay on Your Path to Prosperity

1. I realize that I am in this world for a good reason.

2. I have immense gratitude for my blessings. The more thankful I am, the more I receive.

3. I am aware that nobody is perfect, and I make a unique contribution to this world.

4. I acknowledge that failure is the secret ingredient of success.

5. I am a loved, happy, and valuable human being.

6. I control my attitude toward life to create my reality.

7. I accept responsibility for my actions and circumstances.

8. I do not condemn myself and others. I don't accept insults, and I ignore condemnation.

9. Blaming others for my shortcomings and problems is not my style.

10. I am productive by not procrastinating and doing things on a priority basis.

11. I get fascinated, not frustrated, with unexpected situations.

12. I accept every setback as a springboard to bounce back.

13. Persistence acts like glue for my commitments. I am patient.

14. I am disciplined and committed to my life objectives.

15. I love to take initiative to grow, advance, and make progress.

16. I keep myself excited by thinking positive, keeping my posture erect, and maintaining enthusiasm in all my actions.

17. I am kind, warm, and grateful toward others.

18. I am happy to release money, and it comes to me in increasing amounts.

In your journey to attain a successful, abundant life, you will also come across abundant distractions. Many people lose their grip on success by wasting energy fulfilling others' needs, demands, and expectations. You deserve to live the rich and fulfilling life you desire. Steve Siebold says, "The actions of world-class people are congruent with the size and scope of their vision. Congruence between your vision and your action will determine whether you are a visionary or a daydreamer."[46]

You need to acquire the quality of taking initiative—taking the right action without being told to act by someone else. Acting upon certain knowledge and ideas takes place due to the successful habit of execution. By staying excited, you will energize the execution part of your plan. A prosperity mentality is the capacity to visualize yourself as abundant even if you have little at present. This extraordinary capacity provides strength and courage to take initiative.

Prosperity flows from positive energy, ideas, and action. You will be successful in developing dynamic energy if you stay enthusiastic and face life's upheavals calmly. The energy you transmit to the world is the indication of the type of energy originating within you. Energy is invisible, and it enables humans to act. Therefore, you constantly need positive energy, constructive imagination, and willingness to act in the right direction to activate your success factors for financial

---

[46] Steve Siebold, *177 Mental Toughness Secrets of the World Class: The Thought Processes, Habits and Philosophies of the Great Ones* (London: London House Press, 2010), 240.

abundance and prosperity. *Develop dynamic energy, and you will prosper.*

There is no limit to your capacity for success except that which is imposed by you. Any experience you have on your journey of life will make you more profound, and your current activities will impact your future. The profoundness of your experience is for your benefit, while the impactfulness of your deeds is for others' benefit. Develop the habit of winning and succeeding in your life to make it impactful.

The burning desire to have financial abundance is the internal motivating power that constantly propels you. Recognition, appreciation, and accolades are your external motivational factors. You should be motivated to live in this world and pursue a worthy cause. Your achievement and contribution to the world will outlive your life.

Chapter 12
Take Action to Earn Money

This chapter is about the actions you will take based on your transformed mindset. Some actions might go against your old habits or not according to what society tells us. But that's the way to come out of your old situation and step into your new prosperous world. You are here to get fulfilled with money.

One of the most valuable assets you have is your ability to earn money, and this grows immensely with the contribution of your personal and professional networks. Invest your time networking with truly prosperous people so that you are able to strategically place yourself in settings of abundance-oriented functions, events, and social gatherings. You will benefit from a symbiotic and synergistic relationship of give and take.

To enjoy abundance, you need to be willing to make a decision and take full responsibility for the outcome. In other words, you don't blame others for your circumstances. The consignment of responsibility involving your worthy cause will not break you; instead, it will strengthen you. The more versatile you strive to become, the more easily you will navigate through the journey of life.

The previous chapters were designed to lay the groundwork, give you a foundation for attracting money, and help you develop a prosperity mindset. I highly recommend spending more time and effort on your foundation. This is very important because manifesting money—or anything else outside of you—is dependent on what is inside of you. Your mindset about money and abundance will help materialize things in your life.

Action is as essential to implement your prosperity blueprint as the ignition switch is to any motor. Action causes the transfer of energy and growth. Knowledge, when executed and acted upon, becomes useful, providing respective results. The application of knowledge is powerful. You might have profound knowledge about creating wealth, but it will not make you rich unless you apply the knowledge.

I love the slogan "Just Do It"[47] from Nike. To accomplish abundance, you must act on your prosperity blueprint. Your actions create momentum for your moods, so act positively to gain courage. Act joyously by learning and taking interest in your task. Just do it, and keep doing it, to leave no excuse for an undone task. Be in the state of receiving to get your share of success. Commit to doing whatever it takes to make yourself rich, and then just start and stay persistent.

Your purpose or work should be attached to the attainment of abundance, and you should consistently focus all your mental power, capability, and individual strength to realize your prosperity goal. Put your thoughtful purpose on paper and focus on it. Make combined use of your ability, experience, resources, and know-how to act upon the task at hand.

Money earned is the result of some action. Your actions are the result of your connection with your ideas, habits, and beliefs. Ideas are just wishful thinking without execution. So, act on your ideas and

---

[47] https://en.wikipedia.org/wiki/Just_Do_It

thoughts before they die away. Daymon Aiken says, "Ideas are flighty things. That which now seems perfectly clear may later get away from you. Make a habit of jotting down ideas as they occur to you. And any action takes place only after a thought occurs in the mind. Although many of the ideas will not work out, they may suggest other thoughts."[48]

Remember to appreciate others' ideas. If you criticize or condemn anybody's idea, you will tend to distract from your own creativity. Besides your personal effort, you also need to seek help from other like-minded people. Collaborating with a team of helpful people is very compatible with achieving worthy goals leading to prosperity.

Money is the most important aspect of prosperity, and it can be exchanged for other physical things. *Increasing cash flow into your bank account is the expression of your creativity to connect with those who will give you money in exchange for your goods or services.* You can be creative about multiplying your sources of income, and for this you need to have your imagination stimulated by the possibilities available out there. Your wealth consciousness can be stimulated by your association with wealthy people. Creativity increases your capabilities to see or imagine varied solutions to life's problems.

There is never a lack of money in the universe for a person who can solve major problems. Any job, business, or enterprise is based on providing some kind of solution. The more capable you become of solving major problems, the greater compensation you will attract. Author William Feather said, "Wealth flows from energy and ideas."[49] When you aim to manifest richness in all areas of your life, you will have clear objectives that will eventually keep you moving forward.

---

[48] Daymon Aiken, in Mack R. Douglas, *How to Make a Habit of Succeeding* (New Orleans: Pelican Publishing Company, 1994), 62.

[49] https://www.brainyquote.com/quotes/william_feather_122877

People with a lottery mentality indulge in wishing and begging for more money. As an individual with a prosperity mentality, you work on adding value to solve major problems, and the effect of higher compensation will then materialize. Don't think of work in terms of time spent; instead, enjoy your work and treat it as a measure of overall productivity. Tim Ferriss says, "Focus on being productive instead of busy."[50]

What is the average belief about money in our society today?

Let's probe into what advice you might get from friends, family, and experts.

- Save more money.
- Buying coffee every day costs a fortune.
- Don't spend so much.
- Don't carry credit cards.
- Stop spending to entertain yourself.

All this advice will help you save a little bit more money and can prevent you from getting into debt. I totally agree with it, but I am trying to help you understand the true mindset hidden in all of this kind of advice. The common factor is *scarcity*. Our society tells us to focus on scarcity.

Now, I hope you understand where I am heading. When you are given traditional advice, it doesn't mean that your family and friends don't like you. In fact, they love you and want to protect you because they are also in the same situation. People advise according to what they believe in.

You'll generally hear scarcity-infected advice when you are trying to get out of debt, or you want to amass a huge amount of savings. Such advice doesn't contribute toward wealth creation though. This is the reason most people don't enjoy financial freedom.

---

[50] https://www.vanguardngr.com/2021/01/focus-on-being-productive-instead-of-being-busy-tim-ferriss-advice-for-2021/

I am here to let you know that this is not the way rich people become rich. This is not the advice I am going to incorporate into your mind. My job is to shift your thinking, enrich your belief, and change your behavior toward money. You can become successful in creating a prosperous lifestyle if you get into the habit of learning, growing, and becoming. See yourself as a cocreator; create your own opportunity. This realization will prevent you from passively waiting for an opportunity and getting frustrated. Put your heart and soul into succeeding.

Seizing the opportunity and getting into the game should be your preference over the fear of losing. Be willing to opt for growth over security. Be solution oriented. It's necessary to learn how to feel comfortable while performing in an uncomfortable situation in order to habitually replace fear with faith.

It's easy to have a sense of prosperity if you are wealthy. Most of the limiting beliefs about money that people harbor in their minds are not imposed by others; they give rise to these beliefs themselves. It costs a fortune to allow self-imposed limitations about wealth, money, lifestyle, abundance, and prosperity. Author and philosopher Ayn Rand said, "Wealth is the product of a man's capacity to think."[51]

The key to becoming wealthy is *creating multiple sources of money.* Yes, you read that right. The essence of wealth is making new money and manifesting more money. Your life will be fulfilled only when you start enjoying an abundant life and stop focusing on scarcity.

When you keep thinking about holding on to what you have and holding yourself back from the things you want to do, you are denying yourself the things you want to have. This mentality is actually a scarcity mindset and generates negative energy. This lower vibration will always keep you in a position of lack.

---

[51] https://www.goodreads.com/quotes/23473-wealth-is-the-product-of-man-s-capacity-to-think

Our society is conditioned to view situations as problems. In order to enjoy abundance, I decided to become solution oriented. On every possible occasion, I engaged in realistic thinking so I could find solutions and leap forward. Realistic thinking helps develop a practical plan by simplifying practices and procedures.

My hope is that you also want to manifest abundance and prosperity in your life and are starting to believe that you can become wealthy. This is very important because whatever you visualize, you will realize.

So far, you might have struggled and tried hard but still do not have enough. This is not a fun way to live. Can you do anything about your past? No one has the ability to go back in the past. Therefore, it would be better to stop worrying about the past. It's advisable to unblock the flow of positive energy to your life.

The present moment is with you. What are you doing right now? You are learning to develop a prosperity mindset. There is a reason you are reading this book. You had thought about living an abundant life, and the universe has sent this book into your life.

From now on, you should stop worrying about financial struggles, so you do not attract scarcity. You need to start focusing on attracting money from multiple sources in increasing amounts. Forget about cutting up your credit cards and saving a penny here and there. Your new focus will be on your new attitude. *Your new intention will be about earning money from multiple sources.* Start focusing your attention on prosperity.

Remember that wherever focus goes, energy flows. So, at any given moment, generate positive energy about attracting money. *The secret to a wealthy life is enjoying life by attracting more money. A preoccupation with saving, saving, and saving by limiting yourself leads to scarcity thinking.*

Now, you might be thinking about how to create new sources of money. *Financial freedom can mainly be achieved by passive income and multiple streams of income.*

What Kind of Energy Do You Generate When You Think of Having Multiple Income Sources?

- How do you feel about having multiple sources of income in your life?

- What do you feel when you think about creating passive income for yourself?

It's vital that you do the assessment on yourself as a self-healer and become aware of your thoughts about financial freedom. It's important to review your mindset about creating multiple sources of income in your life.

If you are relaxed when you think about multiple sources of income, you will generate positive energy. That's all you need right now. Marcus Aurelius said, "Very little is needed to make a happy life; it is all within yourself, in your way of thinking."[52]

Prosperity thinkers are solution oriented and always have hope for a better future. Those who hone the art of prosperity thinking can attract abundance even in difficult circumstances. Right thinking can navigate you to a higher level by helping you solve problems, create opportunities, earn more, and remain happy.

On the contrary, if you are anxious and worried, it means you have limiting beliefs about yourself.

What Limiting Beliefs Are Coming Up in Your Mind?

- Are you worried that you don't know how you can earn a new income?

- Are you scared that you have to work very hard to make a lot of money?

- Do you believe that you are not smart enough to have financial freedom in your life?

---

[52] https://www.brainyquote.com/quotes/marcus_aurelius_386395

You need to deal with any limiting belief and fix it as soon as possible. Getting rid of limiting beliefs creates a positive mindset and makes the mind fertile to grow plants of possibilities. I see it as my responsibility to help you do that. My only intention is to move you toward achieving financial freedom.

I have a vested interest in your growth because you have invested in this book. I want you to believe that you have access to one of the best tools for transforming your mindset to get fulfilled with money.

So, if you have recognized that your feelings about multiple streams of income are leaning more toward the negative side, then it's time to fix it. It's easy. Just say to yourself time and again that this universe does not discriminate. Affirm that you are born to be rich. *Believe that you also deserve prosperity and it's on its way to you.* Have faith that if some people can do it, you can too. Once you shift your mindset, anything is possible.

Until now, we have covered much of the internal foundation of creating financial freedom. Let's now go over the external stuff—the reflection and expression of what you think and believe internally.

Statistics say that about 20 percent of the population own about 80 percent of the wealth in this world. This is because most people (i.e., almost 80 percent) are trading their time to earn active income. Active income is basically the income you have to work for each time. Whenever you stop working, your active income stops. Active income includes wages, salary, commission, and margin. There is limited growth in active income. If active income is the only source of income in your life, you will find it very difficult to gain financial freedom.

You might be earning active income from a job or any kind of small-scale self-employment. In either case, you trade your time for money, and you don't have much chance to enjoy the freedom of time and money. Everybody has only twenty-four hours in a day and two hands to work with. Out of these twenty-four hours, you can utilize only a certain number of hours to work and earn money. There is a limitation about how many hours you can really work.

With a job, your working hours are decided by the supervisor, manager, or employer. With self-employment, you can decide to work as much as you want because you are your own boss, but eventually, time runs out. If you as your own boss work more than fifteen hours a day in order to earn more money, eventually the time will come when your body starts giving up and you will burn out. *This results in a limitation of growth in active income.*

Besides limited growth, there is also insecurity involved in active income. Your income stops as soon as you are unable to go to work in your job or your self-employment. *Because of limited growth and insecurity in active income, you have much less chance of becoming wealthy and financially free.*

You Might Be Wondering

- How can I have freedom of time and money?
- How can I earn money through multiple streams?
- How can I become part of the top 5 percent of income earners?
- How can I earn money through passive income?

Some of you might be thinking: *Is it possible for me to get out of this active income trap and have passive income to become financially free?* The answer is a big YES. Yes, you can change the way you are earning money. Yes, you can change your destiny. Yes, you can have full control of your time and money.

To change your financial situation, you first need to change yourself. *You receive in proportion to what you become.* The universal law of cause and effect will work in your favor if you start working on improving your inner world. You need to do things differently in order to get different results. The top earners also have the same twenty-four hours a day that you have, but they do things differently.

Start working now to create businesses. You are destined to have multiple streams of income by developing a business. *A business is a moneymaking tool where a system is in place to generate income.* If some people can earn passive income, you can too.

Important Points to Ponder

- Are you mentally prepared to accept that you deserve passive income?
- Do you believe that you deserve a better quality of life?
- Do you accept the fact that you were born equally as blessed as other successful people?

Remember, your outer manifestation is the expression of your inner thought process and belief. Wealthy people are not working harder than you. Everybody, including you, is already working hard. Whether you are a laborer, a professional, an office worker, or a sports person, you are working hard irrespective of your profession. Wealthy people do things differently. Wealthy people work really hard during the beginning, and once a source of passive income is set after a few months or years of hard work, they enjoy the freedom of time and money.

You are going to work hard throughout your life, so why not earn seven figures income—or even more? It is totally possible for you to also be part of the top 20 percent of the population. You can make this switch by following in the footprints of wealthy people.

Three Steps for Becoming Rich:

Step One: Wealthy people are good at visualizing and imagining what they want to become. They think big and believe in their dreams and goals. They put their ideas on paper and induce energy into their dreams.

Step Two: Wealthy people look for people who have already achieved something similar and have been successful. They step out of their current association and comfort zone and draw up a navigation blueprint to reach their dream destination. They take immediate action to step into this new world based on their big thinking.

Step Three: Wealthy people refuse to go back to their previous state of mind, previous association, and poor work ethic. They dwell in a new, progressive zone. They become comfortable living outside their comfort zone.

You, too, can achieve financial freedom by following the above steps and working hard in a disciplined way with a wealth mindset. Start thinking big. Many people have the capacity to think big and visualize good stuff, but the majority don't step out of their comfort zones; they don't think outside the box. Or if they do venture out of the box, they don't stay in the new zone for long.

About 80 percent of the population has the tendency to dwell in the same box, in the same zone, and—most importantly—in the same mindset. They keep thinking that one fine day will come when they will do something. Time eventually passes by and after one year, three years, five years, or even ten years, they still find themselves in the same spot.

We all have great ideas of becoming wealthy, of becoming millionaires. We all have unique potential and the ability to provide solutions to people and earn money in return. Many dream of writing a book, starting a business, inventing a new product, or introducing a new concept to a traditional industry. But all those ideas end up being just ideas in most cases.

There are few who energize their ideas by taking action. You need to take massive action to make your dreams come true. You don't need to know and learn everything to become successful overnight. *The most important task is to take the first step, do something about your ideas, and keep moving forward.* You will find the necessary tools, know-how, and appropriate people along the way. As you start moving forward, you can't see around the corner or far away, but as you keep moving, you will see the next milestone.

You simply have to visualize the destination in your mind and start working on it. Once you start doing something, you might fail or experience some setbacks. But you will learn something new or find a new tool so you will overcome any failure easily next time. You will be a few steps ahead on your progressive path. *The universe will conspire to help you if you take action with complete belief and faith in yourself.*

Time is a nonrenewable resource. Whether you stand still or run, time never stops. You have a limited amount of time to live. Since you are already living some kind of life, why not live your best life now? What is holding you back from becoming the best version of yourself?

Shift your mindset from doing one day to doing today. This new thinking will fill you with instant energy. Start today with whatever you have right now. Whatever knowledge and tools you have today, start doing something and begin moving. *Once you start, never stop. Just moving little by little creates momentum, and eventually moving becomes much easier.* Taking the first step is crucial.

It takes a lot of mental courage and strength to start doing what you envision doing. The time has arrived to start working on things. Don't create limiting beliefs and hurdles that prevent you from moving forward. Don't be in the illusion of scarcity.

Some Common Obstacles

- I don't have any money.
- I don't know the right people.
- I don't have time.
- I don't think I can do it.
- I'm not smart enough.
- I don't have a good voice.
- People don't like me.
- I am too fat (thin, short, tall).

- I am black (brown).
- I am a woman.
- I am a man.
- I am a divorcee.
- I have kids to take care of.
- I have a full-time job.

At this very moment I am challenging you to convert your weakness into your strength:

- Your poverty should be your reason to become rich, not your excuse to be at the mercy of others.
- Your children should be your reason to win, not your excuse to stay pathetic.
- The fact that your partner quit on you should be your reason to move forward, not your excuse to live a miserable life.

Whatever your excuse, you need to start seeing it as a valid reason to rise above and perform at a higher level.

High achievers are not born with golden spoons in their mouths. Successful people are not born successful. *Common people learn to see the obstacles as stepping-stones and become successful people.*

Now it's up to you to decide what you want. If you suddenly find yourself up against a wall, do you expect the wall to move out of your way—or do you change your course and take a different route to reach your destination?

Your dream goal should always stay firm in your mind, and when you come across any obstacles, you should either remove the obstacle, change your course, utilize different tools, associate with different people, or learn different skills. You should do whatever it takes to reach your destination. Repeat this statement: "If it is to be, it is up to me." Repeat this statement again and again to cement in your mind that you are responsible for your success. *It's you who can transform your life. The universe will assist you only if you take action.*

Whatever you are doing right now to earn a living, keep doing it, and create a new source of income on the side. Think about doing something related to your passion. When you indulge in doing something you love and you start making money, you won't have any problem working extra hours.

In the beginning you will need to sacrifice something to work on other things. Maybe you can give up on watching TV, start waking up an hour earlier, or listen to some learning materials while driving.

You are here to increase your wealth and become fulfilled with money. Do you know exactly how much more money you want in the coming months or by the end of this year? Don't say a lot. Be specific and determine how much you want to make. *Write the amount of money on paper and put a date by when you want it.* Decide, commit, and declare that you are going to make it happen.

Once you set your intention specifically on your goal, the universe will also pay attention and conspire to help you manifest it. *Once your intention and action set the wheels in motion, you will begin to see desirable signals all around, bringing financial abundance in amazing ways.* You will begin seeing ideas and opportunities that were invisible before. Your mind will connect with the things you desire most, and the universe will provide you with all things you actively are working for.

Your intention combined with your motion brings momentum, which in turn helps with manifestation. Having the right intention leads to visualization, and visualization leads to realization. Be mindful that visualization brings realization with the help of action.

You might not always succeed the first time. People might laugh at you at times. *Most, if not all, successful people have failed many times. Average people don't even try as many times as successful people have failed.* Those failures are invisible to us; what we see is only success. Sacrifices are not visible, and when we see the final success, we think that the successful person got lucky or was at the right place at the right time.

But in reality, winners keep working, keep getting up, keep moving one step at a time—and they never quit. Average people quit easily when they fail or face an obstacle. Remember, quitters never win, and winners never quit. When achievers meet a setback, they get up again, learn the lessons, course correct, and move on. Constant course correction is part of the journey to achieve goals. While driving, we always keep our hands on the steering wheel and keep doing course corrections so that we don't veer off the road, and eventually we reach our destination.

Once you start doing things differently and start living outside the box, some of your friends and family might not like it. They might pull you back out of love or for safety reasons. They want you to be part of the crowd for their own sense of security or possibly for some negative reasons.

When you start making a lot of money and become wealthy, you might end up losing some of your friends, but you will make some new friends along the way. You will be part of a new association. *Any time you want to move up to the next level, start associating with people who are already at that upper level. You will develop a next-level mindset and manifest more into your life.*

I hope this book is helping you to think and act differently. I really encourage you to stretch your imagination and envision how good your life could be. I want you to shed all the limiting beliefs that have taken root in your mind due to your past experiences. I want you to see yourself just as privileged as other achievers are.

It's important to raise your self-esteem and start living on your terms. Remember that the universe never discriminates between you and others. It's only *your* thinking that creates limiting beliefs. Wayne Dyer wisely said, "The only limits you have are the limits you believe."[53]

---

[53] https://www.goodreads.com/quotes/8011971-the-only-limits-you-have-are-the-limits-you-believe

So, decide on the amount of money you want to make by a certain date. Make sure the amount and date are written down on the paper. *Anything written has more energy and more life.* The amount should be really big per your current thinking. This will prove that you are thinking outside the box. Start believing you can materialize the money you want to earn; start believing in the universe. Dale Carnegie said, "If you want to be happy, set yourself a goal that commands your thoughts, liberates your energy, and inspires your hopes. Happiness is within you. It comes from doing some certain thing into which you can put all your thought and energy."[54]

Ever since I read the great book *Think and Grow Rich*, I've followed the instructions by author Napoleon Hill to set and achieve any goal in my life. Therefore, here I quote the exact word-for-word six-step instruction he gives.[55]

The method by which *desire* for riches can be transmuted into its financial equivalent consists of six definite, practical steps:

1. Fix in your mind the exact amount of money you desire. It is not sufficient merely to say, "I want plenty of money." Be definite as to the amount. (There is a psychological reason for definiteness.)

2. Determine exactly what you intend to give in return for the money you desire. (There is no such reality as "something for nothing.")

3. Establish a definite date when you intend to possess the money you desire.

4. Create a definite plan for carrying out your desire, and begin at once, whether you are ready or not, to put this plan into action.

---

[54] https://www.azquotes.com/quote/786282
[55] Napoleon Hill, *Think and Grow Rich* (New York: Penguin Books, 2005), 22.

5. Write out a clear, concise statement of the amount of money you intend to acquire. Name the time limit for its acquisition. State what you intend to give in return for the money and describe clearly the plan through which you intend to accumulate it.

6. Read your written statement aloud, twice daily, once just before retiring at night, and once after rising in the morning. As you read, see, feel, and believe yourself already in possession of the money.

The instructions given in the sixth step are crucial. I followed the instructions described in the above six steps in order to achieve my goal of owning two businesses, one in the hospitality industry and the other in the financial industry.

I will illustrate a sample of my written statement to earn a certain amount of money in the hospitality industry as follows:

> *By March 31st, the end of the first quarter of the year, I will have a profit of $100,000, which will come to me in various amounts on a continuous basis. In return for this money, my business will provide the best possible quality products and the most efficient service of which we are capable. I believe I will have this money in my possession. My faith is so strong that I can now visualize this money before my eyes, and I can touch it with my hands. It is now awaiting transfer to me in the proportion that my business delivers the products and services. My plan is in place, and I execute the plan daily.*

Your goal to be prosperous is worthy to pursue, and your success lies in the persistent achievement of challenging milestones. There must be a conscious commitment to your potential in order to achieve your goal. *It's important to take action and make things happen to generate new income. You need to involve yourself in the right kind of activity.* If you don't change your activity, you will not get different results.

Ask yourself some questions. Have you ever thought about making additional income? What ways are you aware of for earning extra money? How can people earn additional income?

How many ways of earning money can you write? Take some time and do some thinking on paper. Try to think about as many ways as possible of earning money. Don't allow any limiting belief to block your thought process. I am sure you can come up with at least ten new ways of earning money. I'll cover many other ways of earning new money in the next chapter.

Right now, what kind of feelings are you generating by thinking of the many sources of earning income? Are you a little bit uncomfortable, scared, or excited?

To start with, it's a good idea to keep your current job so you'll have some kind of stability and security. At the same time, you should be mindful that you are looking for new sources of income for yourself.

Have you ever thought about monetizing your passion? Can you think about a way you could earn money doing the things you are passionate about? When you earn money by doing something you love, manifesting money will not feel like work. Sometimes you will come across wonderful ways of making passive income, but initially you might feel like it is not for you. In most cases, you need to step out of your comfort zone and develop passion for doing new things to manifest faster.

When you adopt new thinking, it becomes easy to change your actions and get new results. You want to invest your time in doing something that has the potential of earning passive income. In the beginning, you will need to work hard, change your schedule a bit, learn new skills, practice time management, and be patient. Once the groundwork is done, money will flow freely into your life.

Today it's easier than ever to learn new things. If you don't know how to do something, don't worry. *Being willing to do something significant is more important.* You can learn many new things for free with the help of Google and YouTube.

As long as you are aware of what to do, the "how to do" part will take care of itself. *As soon as you decide to make adjustments in your current routine in order to create a new source of income, the task will become easy.* There is a lot of power in a made-up mind.

Rosa Parks said, "I have learned over the years that when one's mind is made up, this diminishes fear; knowing what must be done does away with fear."[56]

Initially, you will be required to work extra hours to set up your new routine and schedule. But once the new schedule is structured, everything will start rolling forward without much effort. Money from new sources will start flowing into your life, and you will taste success. The more passive income you generate, the more time freedom you will have. Before you know it, you will be fulfilled with money the way you've always wanted. Time freedom and money freedom are the greatest freedoms you can create for yourself.

So, before moving on to the next chapter, I will challenge you to complete three tasks:

1. Think of and write down at least six ways of earning new income.

2. Write down any obstacles that pop up in your mind.

3. Write down the possible solutions to your obstacles.

My suggestion is to invest some quality time in performing this task. It's important to do the inner work. This will build your foundation. Don't allow your limiting beliefs to overpower you.

Remember, remember, remember: Take responsibility for your transformation. Be solution oriented. Believe that the universe will

---

[56] https://www.brainyquote.com/quotes/rosa_parks_390344

conspire to provide you with everything you think of and act on. Set your attention on the right things, have the intention of achieving abundance, and live with an attitude of gratitude. Believe in yourself and get fulfilled money-wise.

Chapter 13
Embrace Failure and Improve Self-Esteem

Winners and losers react in different ways when they fail. Winners learn and bounce back, while losers get crushed by failure. Everybody learns to walk by falling down. You learn pretty much anything by trying, making mistakes, learning lessons, and succeeding. This also is the case with learning to become wealthy. You will learn and achieve the goal of attaining financial freedom if you operate with a prosperity mindset.

Every individual is unique. Mediocre people are very emotional about their individuality and too stubborn to change. Prosperous people, while respecting their individuality, focus on the continuous evolution of their personality by learning from other people's positive traits, constructive habits, creative ideas, and growth-oriented thoughts.

A prosperity mindset is all about having an awareness that there is never a lack of resources and wealth in this universe. For wealthy people, the process of being rich is fulfilling, and that's why they don't get bothered by the pain of losing. Winners have deep emotional reasons to keep pushing forward. Anything in life is hard without a strong purpose or reason. There is no success story without failure.

People working with a poverty mentality prefer security over growth and fail to spot the real abundance just ahead of them. Most people stay poor or middle class because they are afraid of failure instead of attempting new things and growing. Playing safe means living a limited life and having a mentality rooted in fear and scarcity. You cannot progress with a mentality of not taking action for fear of making mistakes. Don't get paralyzed by a fear of failure—this tends to create an awareness of lack and poverty.

Failures accepted in a positive way will instill courage and confidence in you. Be willing to fail forward because failures are necessary course corrections on the way to your dream destination. Undertake every activity without paying mental attention to the possibility of failure.

Have faith that you deserve abundance and approach life with a growth mindset, unafraid of anything and confident in manifesting your abundance. Abundance-based consciousness operates with limitless possibilities. According to Shannon L. Alder, "When you settle for anything short of the best life God wants to offer you, then you have been tempted to remain safe and the accountability for not changing your life becomes your prison of regret."[57]

Human Beings Are Emotional Creatures

People with a Prosperity Mindset Exhibit These Eighteen Emotion-based Qualities:

1. They deal with money and wealth positively.

2. They have a high level of hope and optimism.

3. They treat time as an invaluable, nonrenewable resource.

4. They are not judgmental.

5. They are good to others.

6. They are in acceptance mode about their circumstances.

---

[57] https://inspirational-quotes.net/quote/137462

7. They feel good about asking for help if necessary.

8. They are not manipulators.

9. They work hard and pray hard with belief in God or the Universe.

10. They keep any feelings of guilt away.

11. They have developed control over anger.

12. They are well-behaved.

13. They have mental toughness.

14. They don't worry about things that might not happen.

15. They have trained themselves to be happy all the time.

16. They live a cheerful and enthusiastic life.

17. They are easy to get along with and are reliable.

18. They treat others with respect and in return earn a lot of respect.

Have confidence in your ability and have faith in a universal power. High achievers possess the self-confidence necessary to make decisions without fear of failure. Psychotherapist and author Nathaniel Branden says, "Self-esteem is the reputation we acquire with ourselves."[58] When you fulfill the promises made to yourself, you grow your self-esteem.

It's human nature to crave recognition and respect. Everybody feels good about being appreciated. Look for opportunities to be appreciative and kind to others often during the day, and your day will turn out to be blessed and impactful. Prosperous people are not addicted to others' approval. They welcome criticism and conflict as tools for emotional growth rather than suffering from emotional injury.

People perform at different levels guided by their beliefs and how they feel at any given time. Prosperous people possess a high level of

---

[58] https://www.brainyquote.com/quotes/nathaniel_branden_110153

belief in who they are and a solid conviction in what they do. If you have a high level of respect for yourself, you will have high self-esteem and will easily respect others. Solid self-respect gives you an edge, empowering you to do whatever it takes to perform, persevere, and propel yourself to prosperity.

Don't suffer under the influence of self-created excuses such as I am too old, I am too young, I am dark, I am too short, I am from a poor family, I am female, I am male, I don't have enough education, etc. Prosperous people were not born prosperous; instead, they learned to turn their weaknesses into strengths and their liabilities into assets. In fact, the universe never imposes any limitations on what you can or can't do. Every individual has an unlimited supply of untapped power. *Your only obligation should always be to think about what you can do.*

Get emotionally charged with happiness, higher self-esteem, enthusiasm, and an abundance mentality by playing the game of life with like-minded people. It is beneficial to keep replenishing your source of power with rich associations, prosperity thoughts, impactful activities, and joyous memories so you will never be in short supply of anything. Find a group of prosperous and affluent people. Pick and choose your associations and draw psychological power from them.

Chapter 14
Avoid Procrastination

If you desire to be positioned on the progressive path of life, you must take action—and you must avoid procrastination. We all have the ability to manifest great things with simple beginnings. Every time I want to start a new project to add to my abundant life, I get inspired by the Chinese proverb, "A journey of a thousand miles begins with the first step."[59] It reminds me that I must begin my journey to reach my destination. This works the same way for everyone. You need to start working on your task to achieve your goal. Postponing work for some other time is a bad habit.

Your latent abilities tend to resurface on the path of constant progress with the help of the energy that results from taking action. Once you decide to achieve your goal of living an abundant life, it's time to start working on your prosperity blueprint. Once you start, you will advance toward your destination. The force of execution is empowered by the intensity of your passion and burning desire. You will be more confident day by day as you move forward.

---

[59] https://literarydevices.net/a-journey-of-a-thousand-miles-begins-with-a-single-step/

Your goal to become prosperous is hampered by procrastination. You could have started on so many projects, but you kept postponing this due to various reasons. You could have been working toward your dream a long time ago if you had just started. You need to get into action and persist through pain, happiness, suffering, and joy. There is no shortcut on the road to riches. Financial abundance comes with a price tag, just like every other valuable item.

Here Are Six Nuggets that Can Help You to Believe More in Yourself and Aid You in Avoiding Procrastination:

1. The universe is an abundant source of everything.
2. Asking and expecting is the beginning of the manifesting process.
3. Action and perseverance are required.
4. Transitioning through adverse situations is to be expected.
5. The willingness to not quit is mandatory.
6. Receiving graciously completes the manifesting process.

In order to be in the state of *peak performance*, avoid PIC (Procrastination, Indecisiveness, and Complacency). *Procrastination* is delaying an activity that should be done. *Indecisiveness* is the trait of having a hard time making decisions. *Complacency* is a feeling of self-satisfaction while being unaware of some potential defect. Postponing tasks causes laziness, and you will feel guilty for not making a decision when one should have been made. Eventually, you will get used to living in your comfort zone for the sake of safety.

"Courage is the commitment to begin without any guarantee of success"[60] is a quote by Johann Wolfgang Von Goethe, who was a German poet, novelist, and scientist. He also said, "Enjoy when you

---

[60] https://www.goodreads.com/quotes/8957328-courage-is-the-commitment-to-begin-without-any-guarantee-of

can, and endure when you must."[61] It takes courage to embark on difficult tasks and get out of your comfort zone with the intention of gaining growth. Having the courage to start diminishes the effect of procrastination.

Procrastination is mainly caused by emotional factors, laziness, and giving less priority to important tasks. Generally, people don't have adequate control over their emotions and tend to put off the execution of something that should be done. You might have a good idea that potentially could help lots of people and make lots of money, but then procrastination kicks in and you don't take any action on your idea. Procrastination will keep you from living your abundant life.

A procrastinator often chooses to carry out a simpler task and postpone an important task that seems more complex. Sometimes a person stops enjoying the work and consequently avoids it or postpones it. Stress causes the loss of energy and enthusiasm and thus results in skipping the work to be done. Not having not enough resources causes avoidance to do a task too. Whatever the reason, procrastination occurs in all circumstances and leads to a loss of productivity.

Procrastination not only causes low productivity and inefficiency, but a long-term habit of procrastinating also negatively affects one's mental and physical health. Procrastination is a huge hindrance to achieving a truly prosperous life. Even though an important task is avoided, the need for that task to be done doesn't disappear. Newer tasks keep coming up with the passage of time. The procrastinator then gets overwhelmed with the long list of tasks to be done. A stressed mental state and a loss of self-confidence can both occur because of procrastination.

---

[61] https://www.goodreads.com/quotes/2378-enjoy-when-you-can-and-endure-when-you-must

How to Avoid Procrastination

If you are in the habit of procrastinating, it's worth overcoming it. It's better to beat procrastination than to be beaten by it. Procrastination will block your way to prosperity, so it's critical to avoid it.

Practice These Five Rituals to Avoid Procrastination:

1. **Act and start.** Make up your mind that the task at hand is simple and easy to initiate. Once you start, you will proceed further. The task will become even easier.

2. **Use uplifting self-talk.** Always try to focus on the dominant thought of doing the task. Tell yourself that you are excited to do it, you will do it, or you can do it. These uplifting statements will energize you to take the first step.

3. **Know that more tasks are on the way.** Remind yourself that many more tasks will need your attention. You are responsible to do your work. So, you'd better keep finishing the tasks on a priority basis to eliminate an overwhelming list of tasks.

4. **Reward yourself.** The best reward for finishing a certain task will be your elevated self-confidence. Besides this, you can think of some other reward in advance for yourself after completing the job. Basically, you need to be motivated to do the next task and keep up the momentum.

5. **Don't worry about failure.** Don't worry about not producing the optimum result. This kind of fear holds you back from taking initiative or starting to do certain things. Your mindset should be to start at once with whatever resources you have, trusting that you will figure out the rest during the process. You will learn to do it differently next time if you don't get your desired result. Just remember that you are failing forward, not falling behind.

Chapter 15
Different Ways of Earning Money

Hopefully you have read the previous chapters and followed through on everything. This chapter is about bringing your inner thought processes and outer activities together to produce incredible monetary results in your life.

How does it feel now to talk about big money? Are you comfortable and confident to say that you are on your way to becoming wealthy? If yes, then you really are on the road to riches. If you are not confident, reread the previous chapters again and again until you change your mindset positively about manifesting money. That's the only way this chapter is going to be effective in producing results for you.

Wealth creators know that money is earned by solving people's problems. You receive money in exchange for something. The money comes from any idea, product, or service that solves a problem, and the bigger the problem, the richer the payoff. *The bottom line is that you get paid by helping somebody. You make a lot of money by helping a lot of people.*

Wealthy people enjoy their work so much that they keep increasing their expertise, and as a result, they become wealthy.

Prosperous people learn to create their own environment of ongoing learning, growth, and discipline. They are always engaged in productive activities for self-discovery, personal growth, and contributions to society. *Rich people are comfortable talking about making big money not because they are rich—they become rich because they are comfortable talking about making big money.*

Now, let's move from believing to behaving. It's time to take massive action. It's your time now to experience abundance in your life and manifest all that you believe. The profoundness of your experience and the impact of your activities will shape the magnitude of your abundant life.

You won't fall into a state of abundance overnight or without challenges. Like everybody else, prosperous people also have their share of adversity, but they accept that adversity as learning phases on their path to growth. They operate with the least resistance. They welcome struggle as a critical factor involved in moving up to the next level. They train themselves mentally to see light at the end of the adversity tunnel; this is the ultimate habit of being fearless in the face of unseen, undesired circumstances.

Robert T. Kiyosaki, in his book *Rich Dad's Cashflow Quadrant*, explains four ways to produce income:

- Quadrant One: **Employee,** someone who has a job
- Quadrant Two: **Self-Employed,** someone who owns a job
- Quadrant Three: **Business Owner,** someone who owns a system
- Quadrant Four: **Investor,** someone who owns investments[62]

Business owners and investors receive passive income and are rich. They enjoy the freedom of time and money. Business owners have a system in place so the whole moneymaking process keeps running, even in their absence.

---

[62] https://www.richdad.com/the-cashflow-quadrant

Certain people enjoy an abundant life because they have made a commitment to do whatever it takes to grow a prosperous mindset and perform accordingly. They are very consistent because their actions are in alignment with their prosperity thought process. They invest quality time thinking about their goals and planning the action steps for attainment. They then take massive action and continue to move forward. They refuse to be complacent.

The best way to become a millionaire is to create multiple sources of passive income, save money consistently, and grow money with a combination of various investments. It's your life; you're the one who must take action.

I will describe some practical ways of making money. You don't have to be stressed about doing "all the things" to make money. Your passion, hunger for money, skills, and desire to learn will allow you to earn any amount of money. You can start with one way, and eventually you can add others. You might earn only a little from one and a lot from another, but in the end, it all adds up and matters. What problem will you solve for people? Let's discuss the various amazing ways of making money. Earning extra money will change your life. Despite what others say about money, more money in your bank buys you freedom and can provide you with stability and power. Many people say, "I don't care about money"—and they are mostly broke because of their attitude.

Earning Revenue from Multiple Sources Will Bring These Five Benefits

1. The extra money can be saved and invested wisely to create wealth.

2. You won't have to worry about living paycheck to paycheck.

3. You will enjoy a debt-free life.

4. You'll have more opportunities to help others.

5. You can retire early if you desire.

The purpose of this chapter is to spark ideas for ways you can make extra money. It's up to you how much you choose to make. You can make small amounts of quick money by working for a few extra hours or you can max out your time and effort to earn tons of money. Instead of maxing out their potential, many people are tempted to take the easy path of deceiving, lying, stealing, kidnapping, cutting corners at the workplace, and wasting a fortune playing the lottery. They are only robbing themselves of the power, blessings, exposure, character, integrity, strength-producing struggles, and learning experiences needed to manifest abundance.

There is no shortcut to a wealthy lifestyle. Most people don't live fulfilling lives because of their own limiting beliefs and self-deception. Poverty-conscious people are generally poor and don't even realize that they lack a prosperity mindset. No one can have abundance without a prosperity mindset.

There are numerous ways to make extra money legally. Some are traditional, while others are new ways of making money. Many online gigs are considered a new type of career due to the growing demand for services in our digital world. I would focus more on income streams that allow you to be your own boss while having freedom of time and money. Additional jobs, working part-time, and working overtime are traditional ways of increasing your cash flow, but you lose time freedom and may get trapped forever.

Are you aware of what you should be doing with your life? Do you know which career or business you would enjoy? *The ability to sell is the most specialized skill you can master to have a successful and prosperous life.* Selling is not to be confused with the profession of selling. The ability to sell is defined as being able to have an impactful communication with another human being, be it a friend, spouse, child, customer, boss, employee, government official, or any other person. Communication can be done through body language, speaking, listening, or writing—or by merely reading one's mind. The art of negotiation is an integral part of selling; it is the ability to communicate so that the other person accepts your point of view, while also respecting that person's point of view.

Whatever product, service, or skill you have to offer in exchange for money, should meet a need. The demand of the marketplace should be in alignment with your expertise and passion. Once there is a demand and you have what is needed to be supplied, you can figure out how to supply a lot of people so you can make a lot of money. You have to show up and be present in the marketplace, so people are aware of you and what you offer.

Potential clients or customers will be thinking about what you have that will meet their needs before they are willing to give you their money. They will also decide whether they should buy from you or from someone else. That's why what you offer should be of good value for money.

Different Ways to Create Additional Income

Based on your knowledge and passion, you can invest time and money to start a business. The following ideas can get you started:

- **Write a book and/or an e-book.** You can self-publish on Amazon and other platforms. Whether you publish your book with a publisher or self-publish, you can create royalty income. Whenever someone purchases your book, you get paid. Having a book also acts as your business card, so you gain more authority in your field of expertise.

- **Create an online course.** Creating digital products doesn't require a big investment. You can package your expertise and knowledge into an online course and sell it. This is a very profitable business model for online entrepreneurs. You can sell your virtual products to a wide audience all over the world. You can do webinars and other online workshops to drive traffic to your website so you can sell your virtual programs.

- **Teach others what you know.** Start a part-time business in the teaching industry and help others with your expertise.

- **Learn to be a copywriter.** With the proper passion, you can invest time and effort to develop the skill of copywriting.

- **Become a real estate investor.** Real estate is a great way to provide financial freedom. There are numerous books written by successful people that provide the knowledge to start and win the game of making money in real estate. This type of investment often allows you to leverage others' money to work for you.

- **Join a network marketing opportunity.** If you are someone who has always wanted to own a business but has held back due to concerns, network marketing is an excellent choice. Being associated with a reputable, stable network marketing opportunity or direct selling company will give you the feel of entrepreneurship, and you will be able to transform your employee mindset into a business mindset with a low investment. Network marketing companies typically have excellent training in place, so you'll learn while you earn.

  In the network marketing profession, sales associates can recruit other sales associates. They make active income by selling products and passive income by earning commissions and bonuses on their recruits' sales volume. The best part is that there is no glass ceiling; anybody can reach the top irrespective of when they start. This business runs on the same system for everybody.

  Leaders in network marketing have worked really hard to reach the top. You will have the opportunity to learn from businesspeople about the business—not from academics who have never been in business. You will also move into a positive association and culture.

- **Become a public speaker.** When you are passionate about a particular topic, you can speak about it at conferences or events and get paid for motivating others. It takes hard work and persistence in the beginning, but eventually you can become a profitable public speaker.

- **Participate in online surveys.** Certain survey sites collect information about consumers. These companies, which you can find online, pay you for your time and contribution toward their surveys.

- **Have at least one credit card which gives you cash back when you shop.** Money saved is money earned. But don't fall into the trap of having too many credit cards. They charge very high-interest rates if you don't pay them off in a timely manner.

- **Run errands for people who are busy, physically disabled, or elderly.** Some service sites hire part-timers, but you can also start your own business. You can provide services such as grocery shopping, driving clients to doctors' appointments, picking up dry cleaning, or taking care of other errands.

- **Rent out a spare room in your house.** You might take in a college student or someone new to your area. You can also look into becoming an Airbnb host.

- **Rent out your car to make extra money.** Several companies allow you to rent out your car when you are not using it. Each company has guidelines for insurance needs and the roadworthiness of the car.

- **Let your money work for money.** You can deposit any extra money in a high-interest savings account. You can automate your savings; you can designate a certain amount of money to come out of your checking account into a savings account or into an investment account, and you can also create an emergency fund. Spend some time learning how money works. Research various banks and institutions to assess which ones are best. You can also get advice from a financial advisor.

- **Consider investing online with a robo-advisor.** This is an online digital platform that provides automated investment services. The platform uses technology to manage your portfolio, thus eliminating most fees and hidden costs.

- **Invest in life insurance.** You can provide yourself and the next generation with significant wealth by saving with life insurance in a disciplined way. *Consistent saving over time is one of the best ways to create your wealth.*

- **Start a dog-walking business.** This can be a fun way to earn passive income. If you bring on some associate dog walkers, you'll make a percentage of what they make.

- **Become a freelance photographer.** You can offer to take pictures for various occasions, such as weddings, graduations, family pictures, etc. You can also upload your pictures to certain photography sites that will pay you a percentage of the sales if someone buys your pictures.

- **Sell the stuff you don't need or use anymore.** Declutter to make room for what you truly want and need in your life.

- **Start a blog**. If you are passionate about something and love writing, you can learn to make money with a blog.

- **Become a freelance proofreader.** Publishers are often looking for ways to outsource this service.

- **Become a freelance writer.** You can offer to write blogs, website copy, marketing copy, and more.

- **Become a virtual assistant.** Virtual assistants are in high demand and can assist business owners by offering a wide range of online services.

- **Sell your creations on Etsy.** If you are creative with arts and crafts, you can sell what you make on Etsy. From custom-designed T-shirts to personalized gift products and jewelry; there are many creative ways to sell on Etsy.

- **Become a consultant for local businesses.** Helping businesses manage their social media platforms is a sought-after skill in today's digital world.

- **Consider affiliate marketing.** You can set up an affiliate-focused website or send emails to mailing lists of like-minded people about products and services. If you are focused on building a mailing list, please work on creating a relationship with this community. This way you can offer them great offers, products, and services through affiliate marketing, and in return, you'll get a commission.

- **Offer technical support.** If you are a professional web designer or developer, you can make money by reaching out to people who are not tech-savvy.

- **Develop an app.** You can make money if you have the technical skills to create something new and useful for the marketplace.

- **Become an influencer.** Influence marketing requires having a large number of followers on various social media sites.

- **Become a translator or interpreter.** If you know two or more languages, this is a good way to put them to use.

- **Launch your own YouTube channel.** Here's a chance to share your knowledge and passion with a wide audience.

- **Become an Uber driver.** You can decide your own hours and work in a way that fits your schedule.

- **Become a coach or trainer for a specific sport.** This is a great way to monetize a sport you're already passionate about.

- **Become a tutor or start a tutoring business.** You'll be helping the next generation to excel.

- **Start your own podcast.** If you like to converse with people, this can be a great way to share your knowledge and expertise with the world.

- **Become a mentor in any area of your expertise.** Coaching in areas such as nutrition, business, happiness, relationships, and other fields is in great demand.

- **Become a Mystery Shopper.** You'll get paid for shopping and sharing your findings with the required company.

- **Sell your baked goods.** If cooking or baking is your passion, consider selling your home-baked food or start catering on a small scale.

- **Perform beyond expectation in your current employment.** You will eventually get noticed and might even get a pay raise. If not, at least you will have developed a great work ethic that will help you in future endeavors.

An Exercise for You

1. What are your top three choices for making money? Which choice are you most confident about starting with?

2. Start with whatever resources you have right now, knowing that you will uncover new tools and skills on your journey. Prepare your financial blueprint and take action. As you draw up a plan to achieve your goal, you will automatically head in your desired direction. The key is to start. Just thinking will not do any good. *Overthinking will paralyze you but taking action will create more energy for you.* You will be able to see around the corner only if you take steps to reach the corner.

3. Elevate your vibration by understanding the concepts shared in this book and doing something to manifest money. Make sure you are consistent in moving forward. Choose to think big and develop a rich mindset. Washington Irving wrote, "Great minds have purposes, others have wishes. Little minds are tamed and subdued by misfortunes; but great minds rise above them."[63]

---

[63] https://www.quotes.net/quote/43785

4. It's time to move from dreaming to doing, from believing to behaving. Henry Ford once said, "If you think you can do a thing or think you can't do a thing, you're right."[64] Do something productive every day to move forward toward your goal. You've already been working hard. Now you have the concepts, tools, and strategies to work smarter. The more you think and act to attain abundance, the more excited you will become.

---

[64] https://www.brainyquote.com/quotes/henry_ford_122817

Chapter 16
Money Management

Everybody has choices to either play the game of life safely or play it to prosper. This chapter is dedicated to financial literacy for organizing your money. Some people are good at taking care of all the monetary things in their lives, but most people are far behind in planning and organizing their money due to a lack of financial awareness.

If you don't have self-control, good habits, discipline, and a prosperity mindset, get ready to be pushed around in this world. Life pushes everybody around. The majority give up, while a few persevere and prosper because their *excitement of winning is greater than the fear of losing.*

Our society emphasizes spending due to a lack of financial literacy. For example, most of us have credit cards these days, but the majority of us don't understand how compound interest works on those credit cards. Credit cards promote spending over saving.

My goal is for you to be able to understand your finances better and be equipped to prepare your financial strategy. Once you are educated on the basic financial concepts here, you will be more confident and ready to approach your banker and/or financial advisor for their help. In this chapter, you'll learn six vital steps to improve your financial condition.

Six Steps to Improve Your Financial Condition

Step 1: Increase Your Income

Step 2: Manage Your Debt

Step 3: Create an Emergency Fund

Step 4: Proper Income Protection

Step 5: Grow Your Wealth

Step 6: Preserve Your Estate

Step 1: Increase Your Income

The previous chapter provided lots of ideas on how you might create multiple sources of income. Apply what you learned and take action to increase your cash flow. Financial freedom is not only about how much money you make or what material things you have. True financial freedom is the state of your life when all your financial needs can be taken care of by sources of income created by you without worrying about money.

"A job is really a short-term solution to a long-term problem."[65] Paychecks and job security provide temporary relief to counteract increasing expenses, consumer debts, and liabilities. *Decide, plan, and execute without delay the ways you can get started with launching a business or creating a passive income source.*

A poverty mindset says, "I can't afford it," while a prosperity mindset asks, "How can I afford it?" An extra source of income can change your lifestyle for the better.

If you want to be rich, you must learn how money works. I learned the fundamentals of "money working for money" from different mentors, which I will share here for your benefit. Focus on spending

---

[65] Robert T. Kiyosaki and Sharon L. Lechter, *Rich Dad Poor Dad.* (Paradise Valley, AZ: TechPress, Inc., 1998), 45.

money to buy assets, not liabilities, if you want to generate income. There are plenty of educated professionals in our society who are struggling financially mainly because they acquire too many liabilities. They work hard for money, but they don't know how to put their money to work for money.

In order to create wealth, learn to invest in income-generating assets. Money can be your best employee, working 24/7 without calling in sick. Don't allow your money to be lazy by just sitting in a savings account or being diminished by buying liabilities.

Most people want to be wealthy but choose not to be because they think acquiring wealth is too complicated. They don't realize that the biggest financial struggle is lack of discipline and the lack of a personal budget. Create your own budget and be disciplined to follow it. If needed, you can revise your budget from time to time.

A Budget Is Beneficial To

- Make financial planning more stable.
- Develop financial discipline.
- Become aware of your financial situation.
- Reduce unnecessary expenses.
- Increase saving.

Step 2: Manage Your Debt

Consumer debt is a prime hurdle on the way to financial freedom. It's important to invest some time in learning financial concepts and strategies that help reduce and eliminate debt. Borrowed money has to be paid off with interest—either simple interest or compound interest.

There is a powerful concept called the Rule of 72 that shows how interest can work for you or against you. This rule gives an idea about the amount of time taken by money to be doubled in savings. It also shows the approximate amount of time it takes for the debt to double.

Consider this example to understand how the Rule of 72 works:

A client owes $6,000 on a loan, and the interest rate charged is 12% compounded annually. If no payment is made, the loan amount will double to $12,000 in the next six years—72 divided by 12 equals 6.

If $10,000 is saved and invested at the rate of 8%, the savings will double to $20,000 in the next nine years—72 divided by 8 equals 9.

These Four Steps Can Reduce Debt Faster

1. Resist the temptation to use credit cards beyond your capacity. Spending more than you earn is a pretty risky habit. If you have any credit card debt, make your goal to pay this off first because the interest rate is typically very high and com-pounded every year.

2. Make a commitment not to borrow money.

3. Write a list of all the debts you owe. Put the name of the debt, the balance amount, and the interest rate for each one. Pay more toward the debt with a high-interest rate and strive to eliminate it first while still reducing other debts. This will create momentum, self-motivation, and extra cash flow to pay off your debts one by one.

4. Consider debt consolidation if your debt is from various sources and adds up to a big amount. In this scenario, basic debt management strategies won't help. Debt consolidation is basically a form of refinancing where one loan is taken out to cover the other loans completely. It eliminates the number of creditors to pay each month, and the new loan has a comparatively lower interest rate.

Step 3: Create an Emergency Fund

You should always save some money that is easily accessible to cover unexpected expenses like a broken appliance, a car repair, a surprise income loss, or a medical emergency. This acts as a shock absorber for your financial planning and prevents you from borrowing money.

Ideally, you should have three to six months of expenses in an emergency fund. Due to any unexpected loss of income, you should still have enough money to take care of housing, utilities, food, credit card payments, insurance payments, transportation, and other basic expenses.

Step 4: Proper Income Protection

Creating protection for household income is a very important ingredient of sound financial planning. Income protection is achieved through life insurance, critical illness insurance, and disability insurance.

An unexpected loss of income or a reduction of income can occur due to death, disability, or critical illness, and this could prevent your loved ones from maintaining the same standard of living.

Talk to a licensed insurance agent to determine your appropriate insurance needs and decide to purchase the proper protection. This is an important way to prove that you love your family.

A general rule to determine the necessary life insurance benefit amount is to have enough money after an unexpected death to equal approximately ten times the annual household income. A more detailed way to find out the insurance need is as follows:

Add Up the Amount of Money You Need

- Long-term and or/ short-term debt: _____
- Long-term goals (for example, costs of supporting your favorite charity, projected costs for your children's education): _____
- Ten times the insured's annual income: _____
- The amount needed for funeral expenses and final taxes: _____

Add Up the Amount of the Assets You Have

The total of existing assets, such as savings, real estate holdings, and guaranteed investments, etc.

Next, subtract the total of existing assets from the total amount needed. The number you get is the approximate total amount of life insurance you should have.

Your financial situation will determine whether you want temporary life insurance or permanent life insurance. Temporary, sometimes called term, life insurance provides coverage for a specific period, such as between ten to thirty-five years, and it is renewable at a higher rate. Permanent life insurance offers lifelong coverage. It also helps build a cash value that is funded by a portion of the insurance premium. Permanent insurance is a product featuring insurance, savings, and investments.

Again, it should be your priority to meet with a licensed life insurance agent for a thorough evaluation of your needs, so you'll know what type of insurance is appropriate for you.

Step 5: Grow Wealth

When you earn money, how do you spend it? Do you spend it all and are left with nothing at the end of the month? I hope you spend considerable time learning from different sources about how money works and what you need to buy with your hard-earned money to become rich. Accumulating wealth is a time-consuming process, and it is the opposite of get-quick-rich schemes.

People become wealthy not just by chance or good luck or not even just because they are at the right place at the right time. People become wealthy by doing things differently and by applying sound financial strategies in a disciplined way for the long-term.

You, Too, Have an Equal Opportunity to Grow Your Wealth by Doing Exactly What Wealthy People Do

- Create multiple sources of income.

- Focus on savings and investments over both the short-term and long-term.

- Protect your principal amount.

- Outpace inflation by using the right investment products.

- Reduce your taxes legally by implementing the right financial concepts.

- Protect your income through different kinds of insurance.

You can determine how much wealth you have by using the following wealth formula:

WEALTH = Money + Time +/- Rate of Return – Inflation – Tax

Your wealth depends upon how much money you are saving and how you are growing it and for how long. The rate of return can be positive or negative, depending on the type of investment. Inflation is always positive, so your money should surpass the inflation rate to give you an extra return on investment. Taxes can reduce your overall savings.

Money grows if it is used to buy assets. The poor and middle-class work hard for money and end up spending money to buy liabilities, thus losing out on time and financial freedom in the future. Remember, an asset is something you own; a liability is something you owe.

An asset is something that has the ability to produce income for you. Buying assets means you are putting your money to work for money. Some common income-generating assets are income-producing real estate, stocks, mutual funds, bonds, investment-grade metals, and intellectual properties such as business licenses, trademarks, copyrights, and patents. But knowledge is required to earn a return on investments.

A liability is something that can cause expenses for you. Buying liabilities means you are spending your money to increase your expenses. If someone is struggling financially, it means that person— knowingly or unknowingly—is spending money buying liabilities.

Some common liabilities that can lead to financial disaster are high compound interest rates payable on credit cards, car loans, unnecessary mortgages (ones that don't generate investment income), and other consumer loans.

Wealthy people enjoy their money more by saving on taxes legally, using their financial education and awareness. They own personal corporations where they accumulate more assets, and the income is used to pay for their car, phone, gas, travel and accommodation, insurance, gift purchases, eating out with clients, etc. These are legal pretax expenses structured within government rules and regulations. Also, the income tax bracket of corporations is lower than the personal income tax bracket. Study to learn more about the benefits of corporations for proper financial prosperity. Rich people like owning corporations, while the poor and middle class do their best to work for a corporation.

Whether you increase your knowledge and awareness about managing money on your own or seek the guidance of a financial professional, financial literacy has the ability to place you on the path to financial freedom.

Step 6: Preserve Your Estate

Your estate includes all the money and property you own, especially at the time of death. You are the best person to make the decisions regarding your legacy, assets, children, medical conditions, and favorite charities. You don't want to leave it to the government or the courts after you are gone and create a situation of confusion for your loved ones.

You work hard to earn money so you can be happy and enjoy your life. You also earn money to make your loved ones happy. You need to put everything in place in order to preserve your estate.

How to Preserve Your Estate

- Prepare your will. When you don't have a will, it can lead to a chaotic situation.

- Make arrangements to transfer your legacy to your intended heir or heirs.

- Preplan and prearrange expenses for your funeral and final taxes. Don't forget that death is certain—and it costs money.

- Set up power of attorney for your future medical needs and financial needs. This gives someone else the power to take care of you should you become incapacitated.

Seek guidance from qualified lawyers and financial professionals. It seems complicated, but professionals make it simple while you are still alive and in control of your stuff. *Can you imagine how complicated it can get if everything of yours has to be dealt with by other people, the government, and the courts?* It can take months or even years to sort out everything, and most importantly, it could diminish your estate to a considerably lower value after paying all the fees and taxes.

Whether somebody is at the poverty level, part of the middle class, or upper class, the majority work hard during their lifetime. Wealthy people work hard, enjoy their lifestyle, and pass their wealth on to their children, favorite charity, or any worthy cause as their legacy. Many wealthy families lose their wealth in the next generation because their heirs lack proper training, have bad spending habits, and haven't learned sound financial principles.

As this book comes to a close, I'll leave you with some prosperity nuggets:

Some Prosperity Nuggets

- Follow your Blueprint for Financial Abundance and you will be prosperous.

- Believe in yourself and you will be prosperous.

- You will be prosperous if you decide to be.

- Be creative on your way to prosperity.

- Being prosperous will be easy by visualizing yourself as wealthy.
- The faster you grow your prosperity mindset, the wealthier you will get.
- The harder and smarter you work, the luckier you get.
- You deserve prosperity in all areas of your life.
- Prosperity is the road to fully experiencing life.
- Elevate your prosperity consciousness to increase the inflow of money in your life.

Manoj Kumar

Author Manoj Kumar is an entrepreneur. He was born in India and lives in Vancouver, Canada with his wife, daughter, and son. He has done his graduation in India and finished his master's degree in London, England. He started his career working in the hospitality industry and eventually upgraded his knowledge to start a second career in the financial sector. Besides India and Canada, he has also worked in the USA and England helping people.

He is a firm believer that the universe is abundant of everything. There is no shortage of money in this world. The universe has plenty of riches for everyone. Scarcity dwells only in people's mind and not in the universe.

He believes that the prime reason people live in poverty is the lack of prosperity mindset. People who complain about money, don't manifest it. Gratitude towards money creates abundance.

Manoj Kumar is on mission to change people's thought processes about money. Money is just a medium of exchange. Money is neutral. Money has the ability to make you more of what you are. Manoj loves people and uses money to help others.

He coaches people to grow prosperity mindset. He insists on taking massive action to achieve financial freedom but always insists that positive thought is the only seed having potential to grow into the tree of an abundant future.

For more great books from Peak Press
Visit Books.GracePointPublishing.com

PEAK PRESS

If you enjoyed reading *Grow Your Prosperity Mindset and Create Wealth*, and purchased it through an online retailer, please return to the site and write a review to help others find the book.

www.ingramcontent.com/pod-product-compliance
Lightning Source LLC
Chambersburg PA
CBHW071600200326
41519CB00021BB/6815